The Vajra Garland
The Lotus Garden

The Vajra Garland
The Lotus Garden

Treasure Biographies of Padmakara and Vairochana

Translated by Yeshe Gyamtso

KTD Publications
Woodstock, New York USA

Published by:
KTD Publications
335 Meads Mountain Road
Woodstock, NY 12498 USA
www.KTDPublications.org

Distributed by:
Namse Bangdzo Bookstore
335 Meads Mountain Road
Woodstock, NY 12498 USA
www.NamseBangdzo.com

ISBN 0-9741092-6-6

This book is printed on acid free paper.

Contents

JAMGON KONGTRUL LABRANG

DEVOTED TO THE ACTIVITIES OF H. E. JAMGON KONGTRUL RINPOCHE

༄༅། །བདག་ཅག་གི་སྟོན་པ་མཉམ་མེད་ཟས་གཙང་སྲས་པོ་གང་ཉིད་ཀྱི་ཐུགས་བསྐྱེད་སྨོན་ལམ་དུས་སུ་སྨིན་ཅིང་། རྒྱ་གར་འཕགས་པའི་ཡུལ་དུ་རྒྱལ་བསྟན་གྱི་པད་ཚལ་སྐྱེ་རྒུའི་ཕན་བདེ་འཇོ་བའི་གསོས་སུ་ཅི་དགར་བཞད་པ་ན། ཕྱོགས་ཀུན་ནས་སྐལ་ལྡན་བུང་བའི་ཚོགས་རྣམས་དང་གིས་འདུས་ཏེ་དམ་ཆོས་ཀྱི་སྦྲང་རྩི་སྣད་རིགས་གཏེར་ཆེན་ཐུམ་པ་གང་བར་འཁྱེར་ཞིང་རང་རང་གི་ཡུལ་ཕྱོགས་སུ་སྐལ་ལྡན་རྣམས་ལ་བགོ་སྐལ་ཏུ་འགྱེད་པས་མ་ཉམས་རྒྱུན་འཛིན་ད་བར་བྱུང་ཡོད་པ་མཐོང་གསལ་རེད། དེ་དག་གི་ནང་ནས་བོད་ཀྱི་སྒྱུར་ནི་ཆད་ལྷག་དང་སྲེས་ལྷད་མེད་པར་མདོ་སྔགས་ཡོངས་སུ་རྫོགས་པ་སོགས་རྨད་བྱུང་ཁྱད་ཆོས་ཀྱིས་མཛེས་པས། དེང་རབས་ཟུར་གནས་མཁས་དབང་ཀུན་གྱིས་དང་བའི་སོར་མོས་མགྲིན་པའི་རྒྱུད་མང་དཀྲོལ་ཞིང་སྟོད་བསྟགས་ཀྱི་གླུ་དབྱངས་སྒྲོགས་པའི་གནས་སུ་གྱུར་པ་ནི་རིམ་བྱོན་ལོ་ཙཱ་བ་རྣམས་ཀྱི་བཀའ་དྲིན་ཁོ་ནར་ངེས་ལ།

དེ་ལས་ལོ་ཆེན་བཻ་རོ་ཙཱ་ན་ནི་མཁྱེན་དཔྱོད་གསལ་ཤིང་ཡངས་ལ་འགྲན་ཟླ་བྲལ་བའི་སྒྱུར་གྱི་བཟོ་ཐབས་ལ་མཁས་པ། དཔེར་ན་ཡུང་བྲུའི་བུ་གར་ནམ་མཁའ་བཙུད་པ་དང་། རྒྱ་མཚོའི་ཆུ་བུམ་པར་བཙུད་པ་བཞིན་ཟབ་རྒྱས་ཀྱི་ཆོས་མཚོ་ཆེག་གི་བུ་གར་ལྷག་མེད་དུ་བཙུད་པའི་འཕྲུལ་ཐབས་ཀྱིས་ཀུན་གྱི་ཡིད་དབང་འཕྲོག་པས། ཕྱིས་བྱུང་ལོ་ཙཱ་བ་ཀུན་གྱིས་གཙུག་རྒྱན་དམ་པར་བཀུར་ན་ད་ལྟ་རྒྱལ་བསྟན་རྫོགས་པར་སྤྱོད་པའི་སྐལ་བཟང་འདི་སྐྱེ་མཆོག་དེ་ཉིད་ཀྱི་བཀའ་དྲིན་དུ་ངེས་ལ། དེང་སྐབས་དབྱིན་སྐད་སོགས་སུ་གསུང་རབས་ཕབ་སྒྱུར་བྱེད་པའི་སྐལ་བཟང་འདིར་སྐྱེ་མཆོག་གང་གི་རྣམ་ཐར་ལ་མིག་ལྟོས་ཡར་ལྟ་བྱས་ནས་རྗེས་སུ་སློབ་པའི་དུས་སུ་བབས་ན། ད་ལན་ཀརྨ་ཏྲི་ཡཱ་ནའི་དཔེ་སྐྲུན་ཚོགས་པས་བསྟན་ལ་དགའ་བའི་ལྷག་བསམ་གྱིས་རྣམ་ཐར་འདི་ཉིད་དཔེ་སྐྲུན་གནང་བ་ནི་སྐབས་བབས་དུས་མཐུན་གྱི་མཛད་བཟང་བླ་མེད་དུ་མཐོང་ནས་རྗེས་སུ་ཡི་རང་དང་བསྟན་འགྲོར་ཕན་རླབས་ཆེ་བའི་སྨོན་འདུན་རྩེ་གཅིག་ཞུ།།

འཇམ་མགོན་ཀོང་སྤྲུལ་བློ་གྲོས་ཆོས་ཀྱི་ཉི་མས།

སྤྱི་ལོ་༢༠༠༥ ཟླ་བ་༨ ཚེས་༡༥ ཉིན་ལ་བ་བཀའ་བརྒྱུད་ཐེག་ཆེན་གླིང་བཤད་གྲྭ་ནས།

Through the ripening of the benevolent aspirations of our Teacher, the peerless Buddha Shakyamuni, Buddhism initially flourished in India, and was like a lotus garden created there for beings' benefit and delight. Fortunate beings naturally gathered from all directions, like bees coming to collect nectar for honey. These beings became like vases filled to the brim with the treasure of dharma, which they subsequently translated into their native languages.

We can clearly see even today that it was through their sharing of dharma with the fortunate people of their various lands that Buddhism still exists as an undiminished, living tradition. Among these translations, those into the Tibetan language were beautified by the inclusion of both sutra and tantra, and were distinguished by freedom from error, addition, and omission. Today, all impartial scholars praise these translations, playing the lutes of their voices with the fingers of faith. All of this is solely due to the kindness of the various translators who have appeared throughout Tibetan history

Among them, the great translator Vairochana possessed a vast and brilliant intellect. His skill in translation was peerless. His ability to put the vast and profound ocean of dharma into words was as amazing as someone fitting all space within a mustard seed or all the water of an ocean within a vase. All subsequent Tibetan translators have placed him above them as the jewel on their crowns. It is definitely due to the kindness of this supreme being that we still have the good fortune to practice the complete teachings of Buddhism.

Nowadays the teachings are being widely published in English and other languages. It is time therefore for us to consider and emulate the example of this supreme being. Karma Triyana Dharmachakra Publications is publishing this biography through their benevolent concern for the teachings. I consider this both excellent and timely and rejoice in it. I also offer my one-pointed prayer of aspiration that this bring vast benefit to the teachings and to beings.

Written by Jamgön Kongtrul Lodrö Chökyi Nyima on September 15, 2005 at the college of Kagyu Tekchen Ling.

Translator's Introduction

The two biographies translated here are treasures revealed by Jamgön Kongtrul Lodrö Taye (1813-1899), the renowned master of the traditions of accomplishment and learning. "Treasures," called *terma* in Tibetan, are teachings and other material concealed for the benefit of the future, and designed to be discovered and revealed by the rebirth of either the writer of the treasure or one of his or her disciples. Jamgön Lodrö Taye was an emanation of the translator Vairochana, the subject of the second of the two biographies. Vairochana was a disciple of Guru Padmasambhava, the subject of the first biography.

There are many types of treasure, but the most common varieties are physically concealed treasure and mentally concealed treasure. Physically concealed treasure can include earth treasure, lake treasure, sky treasure, and more. Sometimes, for the sake of simplicity, they are all collectively called "earth treasure." When used in this wider sense, earth treasure includes any treasure that is physically concealed and discovered. Mentally concealed treasure is what is called "thought treasure." It is concealed in the mind of the disciple, and arises from his or her mind when the time of its revelation is at hand.

The two treasures translated here are not specifically identified as either thought treasure or earth treasure; Jamgön Lodrö Taye simply writes that they were "received as siddhi." Since he revealed both thought and earth treasure, this enigmatic remark could refer to either. In any case, both biographies identify themselves as having been written by the great teacher Yeshe Tsogyal, a key figure in the transmission of treasure. She, like Vairochana, was a principal disciple of Guru Rinpoche. In particular, almost all the teachings of Guru Rinpoche concealed as treasure were presented to her as well as to the disciple whose rebirth would reveal them in the future. In many cases, she wrote down the treasures, and it was also often Yeshe Tsogyal who concealed them. In some cases, she herself emanated the treasure revealer (called *tertön* in Tibetan), but even when the tertön has been the emanation of another disciple, the treasure is regarded as having been passed down by her.

Both biographies are partially written in the first person, the narrator being the subject, and partially in the third person. Both end with colophons identifying the final writer as Yeshe Tsogyal. The implication is that she edited and composed the final text of the biographies, incorporating material either spoken or written by the subjects themselves. The texts were concealed in the form of symbol script, decoded by the tertön. Although there have been treasures in which much of the text was written in Tibetan script, it is apparently more common for the original text to be written in "dakinis' symbol script," which can only be deciphered by someone who has already received the lineage of prophetic entrustment. This is usually the tertön, who received that lineage in his or her previous life as Guru Rinpoche's disciple. Sometimes it is another master associated with the tertön. In either case the text must be transcribed into Tibetan before it can be read by others.

In that way, each of these biographies is the work of three individuals. The biography of Guru Rinpoche was written by Guru Rinpoche and Yeshe Tsogyal, and revealed and deciphered by Jamgön Lodrö Taye; the biography of Vairochana was written by Vairochana and Yeshe Tsogyal, and revealed and deciphered by Jamgön Lodrö Taye.

The purpose of these biographies is to inspire the reader. We are encouraged to vividly imagine the deeds of Guru Rinpoche and Vairochana, both so that we appreciate those deeds and so that we understand something of what such beings are. These are the stories of people utterly unlike us in one sense and identical to us in another. We are not emanations of Amitabha or the buddha Vairochana, and can scarcely imagine living in charnel grounds or gaining the siddhi of invisibility. Nevertheless, all of the qualities demonstrated by Guru Rinpoche and Vairochana are said by them to exist within us right now.

This apparent dichotomy is resolved when we consider the Buddhist understanding of the difference between our nature (our potential) and our present state (our limitations). According to Guru Rinpoche and Vairochana, we are in no way inferior to them in nature and are therefore potentially capable of doing everything they have done. However, because we have as yet not freed our potential from the limitations imposed on it by ignorance, our present state is very different from their present state.

This twofold outlook is necessary for these biographies to be fully appreciated. If we were incapable of achieving what these beings have achieved, there would be little point in studying their deeds. At the same time, seeing how extraordinary that achievement is can remind us that we have not yet realized our full potential. Therefore these stories are both uplifting and humbling.

Readers who wish to read a longer biography of Guru Rinpoche may choose among the many accounts of his deeds that have been translated into English. Those who wish to read a longer account of Vairochana's deeds should read *The Great Image*, translated by Ani Jinba Palmo, and published by Shambhala Publications.

Yeshe Gyamtso

*This translation is dedicated to His Eminence
the Fourth Jamgön Kongtrul Rinpoche,
Lodrö Chökyi Nyima*

The Treasure Biographies of Padmakara and Vairochana

Guru Padmakara

The Vajra Garland
A Biography of Guru Padmakara

Chapter One

Birth and Inheritance of the Throne of Uddiyana

EMAHO!
In that realm without division, partiality, or complexity—
The blissful palace of Lotus Array—
Amitabha, the lord of the three bodies,
Decided to dispatch a supreme buddha emanation
To tame the wild beings of samsara,
To eradicate the incorrect views of tirthikas,
And to light the beacon of genuine dharma.

One born of a womb could not tame them.
To tame all gods, spirits, and humans through actions
    of power and force,
One of miraculous birth was needed.
He therefore emanated me, Padma, as the syllable HRIH
From the mandala of his wisdom vajra mind.[1]

I arose enclosed within a passionless lotus

On an island in the stainless, eightfold waters of Lake
   Danakosha.[2]
The flower's measure was that of a chariot wheel.
It blazed with light and splendor.

During the day it rose to the surface, drawn by the
   sun's light,
Beautifying the vast lake.
At night, too, it rose to the surface, resplendent with
   rainbow light.
Although all the other flowers there
Were newly born annually, the old ones replaced,
The udumvara stalk in the lake's center[3]
Remained undiminished with the passing of
   summer and winter.
It remained closed, at which all wondered.

A messenger of the king saw it
And informed his lord.
The king consulted his ministers and commanded that
   it be watched.
The lotus flower was guarded day and night in shifts.

On the tenth day of the Monkey month in the Monkey
   Year the lotus opened.[4]
In its center was a pleasing, handsome boy.
Rainbows appeared in the sky. Flowers fell as rain.
Thunder resounded. The earth shook. Good signs
   abounded.

The great king of the south, disbelieving,

Came to the lake's shore with his courtiers.
He saw the pleasing, lustrous, radiant boy.
Amazed, the king bowed and praised him.

Thinking, "He might be my destined son. I shall
    take him,"
The king tried to reach the island in a boat.
Unable to do so, he returned to his own land.

Danapala, the king of Uddiyana, had no son.[5]
Having exhausted his treasury through long years
    of generosity,
He had gone to an island to search for jewels.
On his way back, he saw the boy.

Saying, "He is my destined son,"
He brought the lotus and the boy on board his ship.
Having reached his palace, the king offered his
    kingdom to the boy.
The king prayed to the wish-fulfilling jewel
    he had found.

All his previous wealth was restored.
The adopted prince lived in the palace for five years,
Ruling the kingdom well in accord with dharma.

From *An Ornamental Garland of Vajras: A Biography of the Guru,* the first chapter: "Birth and Inheritance of the Throne of Uddiyana."

Chapter Two

Relinquishment of the Throne and Residence in the Charnel Ground of Shitavana

At one time while resting in thought
He saw Vajrasattva's face and received this prophecy:
"How could you benefit beings by ruling this kingdom?
Tame all beings through the actions of power
    and force!"

The Guru thought, "I shall do just that!"
He needed to find a way to cast aside the throne,
And thought, "I will manifest yogic conduct,
Displeasing to the lord and his ministers. I will find
    a way to escape."

With that intention, he engaged in yogic conduct.[6]
Most of the mara-ministers, displeased, came to
    a decision.[7]
They went to the king and said,
"The prince is young and his conduct very wild.

If this continues, our country will be ruined.
He must be exiled to another land!"

The king said no, but it did no good;
The prince was taken to the Indian charnel ground called
    Shitavana.[8]
He brought all of its matrikas and dakinis under his
    sway.[9]
He engaged in fourfold union and liberated all the
    vicious.[10]

He turned the dharmachakra for the dakinis for five years.
When he practiced the deities of Amrita Qualities,
He accomplished them, saw their faces, and received
    prophecy.
He became known as Padmagunasambhava.[11]

From *An Ornamental Garland of Vajras: A Biography of the
Guru,* the second chapter: "Relinquishment of the Throne and
Residence in the Charnel Ground of Shitavana."

Chapter Three

Visions of the Faces of Yidam Deities and the Achievement of Siddhi

He then went to Great HUM Rock
With the intention of becoming a great vidyadhara
    of mind.
He practiced the deities of the Authentic Heruka.
He killed all the men that came there and united
    with all the women.

Perfecting yogic conduct, he stayed there five years.
He turned the dharmachakra for the dakinis,
Saw the faces of the deities of Authentic Mind,
And received the supreme and common siddhis
    at once.[12]
He became known as Padmasamyaksambhava.[13]

Then he went to the charnel ground called
    Terrifying Forest.
Living there, he practiced the deities of Yamantaka.

He adorned his body with the eight charnel-ground
    accessories.[14]
Bringing all the dakinis there under his sway, he presided
    as the great master of their feasts.

Perfecting union and liberation, he attained siddhi.
Seeing the face of Manjushri Yamantaka,
He achieved the powers of the twelve great direct actions.[15]
He stayed there for five years with a stupa as a backrest,
And became known as Padmaprajnasambhava.[16]

Then he went to the charnel ground called
    Piled Lotuses.
Living there, he practiced the deities of Hayagriva,
    Lotus Power.
He perfected the activities of union and liberation.
He turned the dharmachakra of secret mantra for
    the dakinis.

Seeing the faces of the deities of Lotus Power,
He received the supreme empowerment of a great
    vidyadhara of speech,
And became known as Padmahayagrivasambhava.
Staying there five years, he accomplished immeasurable
    benefit for beings.

Then he went to the charnel ground called Forest
    of Revenants.
Living there, he practiced the deities of Kila Activity.
He brought all the matrikas and dakinis there under
    his sway,

Empowered them through union and liberation,
and turned the dharmachakra.

Seeing the faces of the deities of Vajrakumara,
He received empowerment to eradicate obstacles and
the hordes of maras.
He stayed there for five years, seven months,
and ten days,
And became known as Padmakarmasambhava.[17]

From *An Ornamental Garland of Vajras: A Biography of the
Guru,* the third chapter: "Visions of the Faces of Yidam
Deities and the Achievement of Siddhi."

Chapter Four

Practice in the Eight Charnel Grounds and Perfection of the Conduct of Union and Liberation

He then went to the charnel ground called Spontaneously
  Arranged
And practiced the mandala of Matrikas' Exhortation.
He ate corpses as food and wore the clothing of the
  dead as raiment.
He liberated all the men who came there and united
  with all the women.

He turned the dharmachakra for the dakinis there.
Seeing the faces of the deities of Matrikas' Exhortation,
He received empowerment to perform boundless
  supreme and common activity.
Staying there five years, he perfected yogic conduct,
And became known as Padma Exhortation Sambhava.

Then he went to the charnel ground called Expanse
  of Great Bliss

And practiced the deities of Mundane Offering and Praise.
He brought under his sway haughty male, female, and
   neuter beings,
Dakinis, and the eight classes of gods and spirits.

He enlisted them as messengers in the accomplishment
   of the four actions.
Commanding them, he placed them in samaya and
   gave them its substance.
He became the leader of all haughty, mundane beings.
He liberated the five poisons and united with the expanse
   of the five bodies.

Seeing the faces of the mandala of Offering and Praise,
   he acquired siddhi.
He stayed there five years, five months, and five days
And became known as Padma Offering Praise Sambhava.

Then he went to the charnel ground called
   Langka Design.
As there were many vicious maras and rakshasas with
   negative aspirations,
He decided to accomplish the power of force that
   eradicates
In order to tame them all.

He opened the mandala of Forceful Mantra,
And remained in the samadhi of direct action.
Through the actions of controlling, burning,
   and casting,
He dealt with all the elementals and maras.

He killed all the males that appeared and united with
    all the females.
He brought them all under his sway.
All negative views were pulverized.

Seeing the faces of the deities of the Powerful Black One,[19]
He received the empowerment and siddhi to liberate
    enemies of the teaching.
He stayed there five years, nine months, and nine days,
And became known as Padma Power Force Sambhava.

From *An Ornamental Garland of Vajras: A Biography of the
Guru,* the fourth chapter: "Practice in the Eight Charnel
Grounds and Perfection of the Conduct of Union and
Liberation"

Chapter Five

His Establishment of the Kingdom of Zahor in Dharma and His Attainment of Mahamudra Vidyadhara

Then Guru Padmasambhava
Went to all parts of India
With the intention of turning the holy dharmachakra.
To all he said, "I will teach authentic dharma!"

Everyone asked him, "Who is your guru?"
He replied, "I am a self-arisen teacher, a buddha.
Although I have no guru, I know authentic dharma."
Saying, "Other than Shakyamuni, there is no
    self-arisen teacher.
This is a mara," they did not listen to his dharma.

The Guru thought, "Although I possess genuine dharma,
Without a guru I will not benefit beings.
I shall rely on many qualified gurus."[20]

At that time there were many panditas and siddhas in India,

Such as Manjushrimitra, Shri Singha,
Vimalamitra, and others,
Who were both learned and accomplished.

Padma relied upon one hundred and eight of them.
He practiced outer, inner, and secret dharma of
    sutra and tantra.
Especially, he practiced secret mantra, the Great Perfection,
The winds, chandali, and the employment of
    bliss-emptiness.

He came to know all of the five sciences.[21]
He understood everything upon receiving the slightest
    instruction.
Having become learned and accomplished,
    he went to Zahor.

The king of that land was called Tsuklakdzin.
He had many queens and ministers, and was very wealthy.
He had no sons, but had one daughter,
Who was called Princess Mandarava.

Possessing all good attributes, she was like a goddess.
Her beauty surpassed that of any other.
The kings of India, China, Li, Kashmir, Jang,
Uddiyana, Nepal, Persia, Gesar, and other lands
Were competing for her hand,
But she refused them all and was unsullied by
    samsara's flaws.

Practicing divine dharma, she lived apart in her own palace.

The Guru saw that she was fit to be a secret disciple
    of bliss-emptiness.
He turned the dharmachakra of great bliss, the four
    joys' wisdoms.[22]
They lived together in perfect happiness.

An itinerant cowherd came there
And heard of this from Mandarava's attendants.
He repeated the news in his home, and eventually
    everyone heard it.
When the king was told, he became enraged.

He commanded, "Punish that monk!
Throw my daughter and her servants into the
    darkest prison!
If we don't keep this secret,
All the neighboring lands will rise up against us.
So punish them without anyone seeing!"

The ministers held a council and sent twenty deputies.
The Guru performed no miracles to resist them.
Behaving like an ordinary person, he was arrested
    by the deputies.

They soaked hot-burning wood in sesame oil.
They bound the Guru tightly and burned him.
Then they returned to their individual provinces.

The princess and her servants were cast into a dark prison.
They were whipped with thorns and made to suffer terribly.
After seven days the king said,

"Bring me a piece of bone from the forehead
Of that barbarian beggar-monk we burned alive."

A messenger was sent. When he reached the place
    of execution,
It was filled with smoke. The fire was still burning.
In its midst was a lake, with a lotus growing in its center.
In the flower's calyx was Guru Rinpoche.

He appeared to be eight years of age, cool, and refreshed.
Amazed, the messenger bowed to him.
He quickly returned and informed the king.
Disbelieving, the king went to see, bringing his queens,
    ministers, and subjects.
It was exactly as they had heard!

All of them—the king, queens, ministers, and commoners—
Apologized regretfully and placed the Guru's feet on
    their heads.
Invited to the palace, the Guru turned the dharmachakra.
The king offered him Mandarava as a permanent
    companion.
The entire kingdom of Zahor was established in dharma.
Everyone there gained mastery of secret mantra's union
    and liberation.

From *An Ornamental Garland of Vajras: A Biography of the
Guru,* the fifth chapter: "His Establishment of the Kingdom
of Zahor in Dharma and His Attainment of Mahamudra
Vidyadhara."[23]

Chapter Six

His Coming to Tibet and the Building of Samye

Then Guru Padmasambhava, father and mother,[24]
Established the entire kingdom of Uddiyana in dharma.
They subdued all the tirthikas at Vajrasana.[25]
At Shravasti they performed various miracles.
They also established all of Kashmir, Li, and Mongolia
In authentic dharma.

Then the Guru went to Tibet, for the following reasons:
Trisong Detsen, an emanation of Manjushri,
Read the testaments of his father and all his ancestors.
During the three previous kings' reigns
Holy dharma had been just introduced.
He thought, "I must seek dharma now!"

He consulted all the ministers of Tibet,
And began to build the Samye Temple as a basis
    for the teachings.

Through the vicious trickery of malevolent elementals
All that was built during the day by humans was torn
    down at night by spirits.

They returned the earth, stones, and wood to their
    original places.
All the ministers said, "It can't be done. Give up!"
The king refused, saying, "If this work is not
    completed,
There is no point in my remaining alive."

It was decided to invite from among the many
    panditas and siddhas of India
One who could subdue the ground and build
    the temple.
Messengers, fleet of foot, were sent to India.
They invited the great abbot, the bodhisattva
    Shantarakshita.

He came to Tibet and performed the ceremony for
    subduing the ground.
Unable to tame it through any peaceful means,
He prophesied to the king,
"This land of Tibet is a borderland of spirits.
The eight types of haughty beings are extremely
    powerful here.[26]
They cannot be tamed by the womb-born or by peace.

"Invite the miraculously born Padmasambhava.
  If he subdues the ground, Your Majesty's wish will
    be fulfilled.

No one else will be able to subdue it."

The king followed this command and sent escorts
    to India.
The great master came to Tibet for its benefit.
On the way he established all of Nepal in dharma.
He brought under his sway all the haughty masses
    of the eight types,
And especially the three samaya-spoilers: Lokmatrin
    of the sky,
The yaksha Gömaka, and the naga Gyongpo.

He established them in samaya and gave them strict
    commands.
He hid innumerable treasures in Nepal,
And gradually made his way to Tibet.
He bound by samaya the nine great spirits,
    entrusting them with treasure.[27]

Reaching Samye, he met the king.
He subdued the ground, and the spirits were
    unable to stop him.
The central temple was built to resemble the
    Glorious Copper-Colored Mountain,[28]
With three stories of different design, surrounded
    by four continents,
Eight subcontinents, and an enclosure.

Humans built by day and spirits by night.
The foundation was dug in the Tiger Year,
And the work was finished in the Male Water Horse Year.[29]

The wishes of the king, ministers, and subjects
were accomplished.

From *An Ornamental Garland of Vajras: A Biography of the Guru,* the sixth chapter: "His Coming to Tibet and the Building of Samye."

Chapter Seven

The Lighting of the Beacon of Dharma in the Dark Land of Tibet

Then Trisong Detsen thought,
"Although the great external temple has been created,
The supports of body, speech, and mind have not.
I shall consult the abbot and the master, and create them."

He created supports of body and mind as the Guru
    commanded,
And requested the translation into Tibetan of the holy
    dharma as the support of speech.
The Guru predicted three translators, Vairochana
    foremost among them.
They were trained in translation and learned it properly.

Many other children were gathered and trained as translators.
They were sent to India and translated much holy dharma.
The Bön traditions with incorrect views were suppressed,
And those with the authentic view further established.[30]

The mahayana of integrated sutra and mantra spread.
Many siddhas, translators, and panditas were invited,
Among whom the Kashmiri mahapandita Vimalamitra
    was foremost.
All the dictates and shastras known in India were
    translated.[31]
The teachings of sutra and mantra shone like the sun.
The teachings of Padmasambhava spread throughout
    Tibet.

From *An Ornamental Garland of Vajras: A Biography of the
Guru*, the seventh chapter: "The Lighting of the Beacon of
Dharma in the Dark Land of Tibet."

Chapter Eight

The Concealment of Treasure in Tibet and the Fulfillment of the King's Wishes

Then, King Trisong Detsen's hopes having been utterly
    fulfilled,
He gave a magnificent banquet.
He offered great wealth to the translators and panditas,
And had them escorted back to their own lands.

He requested the bodhisattva and Padmasambhava
To remain in Tibet. They consented.
The great master went to Samye Chimpu.
The great abbot Shantarakshita resided in the
    central temple.

Eventually, the king was attacked by illness.
Informed of this, the master went to Yamalung,
Where he practiced the protector Amitayus.
After twenty-one days he saw the faces
Of the immortal protector deities.

He sent word to the king, "Come here. I must give
    you the empowerment of life."
However, the impure ministers prevented this.
The king was unable to go; the opportunity
    was lost.
The Guru concealed as indestructible treasure
All the life substances and mandala materials.

The king, without the ministers' knowledge,
Went on horseback to see the Guru.
He asked for the empowerment. The Guru said,
"You didn't come when I sent for you.
The empowerment substances are no longer here.
I concealed the mandala materials as treasure."

Regretful, the king begged for the empowerment.
The master retrieved the life substances from the
    treasure and, empowering the king, said,
"If Your Majesty had received this empowerment
    at the proper time,
You would have attained immortal vajra life.
This was prevented by demonic mara-ministers.
However, through the power of Your Majesty's
    past aspirations,
Your mind was unchanged and you have received
    empowerment now.
This will prolong your life by thirteen years."

He then again concealed the mandala and life
    substances as treasure.
He also traveled throughout the land of Tibet,

And blessed one hundred and eight places of
    accomplishment.
He concealed as treasure immeasurable profound dharma
    and wealth,
Ensuring that benefit for beings will constantly increase.

From *An Ornamental Garland of Vajras: A Biography of the Guru*, the eighth chapter: "The Concealment of Treasure in Tibet and the Fulfillment of the King's Wishes."

Chapter Nine

The Completion of His Benefit for Beings in Tibet, and the Preparations for His Departure

Sometime after that, the king summoned all the
    translators,
With the abbot and the master presiding.
They all performed the accomplishment of
The *Ocean of Dharma, the Collected Dictates*.[32]

Afterward they enjoyed a vast banquet.
It was then time to celebrate the Tibetan New Year.
The master said, "Don't perform the New Year
    celebration."
But the ministers and queens, when consulted, said,
"We are utterly happy and without any suffering.
It would be unfitting to cancel the New Year celebration."

Based on their counsel, the celebration was performed.
They said, "Let there be a horse race and mounted archery
On the right shore of the lake near Samye!"

The master said, "Don't compete in the horse race,"
But the ministers didn't listen and convinced the king,
    who raced.

Lhazang Lupal disliked dharma because of his liking
    for Bön.
Jealous of the king, he hid in the crowd and shot an arrow.
It entered the king through his ribs and killed him.
Everyone thought his horse had stumbled on a root.
While they were still unsure of what had happened,
    the king died.

Mutik Tsenpo ascended to the throne.
He continued the customs and activities of his father.
The great master Padmasambhava,
For the benefit of beings in the future,
Blessed places of accomplishment all over Tibet
And concealed innumerable profound treasures.

In the central and border areas he created authentic temples
And one hundred and eight Mara-Taming Stupas.
On the peak of Mount Hepo near Samye
Guru Padma and Mutik Tsenpo led
An assembly of hundreds of their lords and subjects
In the performance of a hundred and eight ganachakras.[33]

The Guru summoned all the negative, haughty nonhumans,
Who received commands, were placed in samaya,
Vowed obedience, and offered their life essences.
With that, the Guru's taming of disciples in Tibet
Through his actual presence was complete.

Then the Guru thought,
"It is now time for me to tame the rakshasas."[34]

He summoned Mutik Tsenpo and said to him,
"Son, from your childhood up to now
I have given you my blessing and the essence of my heart.
Your mourning for your father is now finished.
The kingdom is happy; the Buddha's teachings flourish.
There is nothing unpleasant; all good things are
    increasing.
My taming of disciples in Tibet through my actual
    presence is completed.
It is time for me to tame the rakshasas in the southwest.
No one other than I can tame them.
If they are not tamed now, the Buddha's teachings
    will be destroyed.
This will cause misery for beings.
So it is time. Son, be well.
Don't forget me. Constantly pray.
Anyone with faith in me is a fit vessel for my blessings.
They are never apart from me. I am here. I haven't
    gone anywhere."

Mutik Tsenpo was displeased and said,
"I could never bear separation from you, master.
I beg you to be compassionate and remain in Tibet.
My father, the king, did not live but passed away.
If you, Guru, also leave and go to the land of rakshasas,
Will not this land of Tibet become an empty place?
Are beings unworthy of your compassion?
I beg you! Don't go! Remain in Tibet!"

The Guru said, "Mutik Tsenpo, listen!
I am the Guru of all beings.
Would you have me impair my bodhichitta?
If the island of rakshasas in the southwest is not tamed,
All beings will be cast into the swamp of suffering.
If they do not even hear the sound of dharma,
What joy, what happiness will there be?
I will not stay. I am going to tame the rakshasas.
If you are able to pray with faith, respect, and interest,
Padmasambhava has not gone anywhere. I sleep at
    your door.
Each morning and evening I will come with the rays of
    sunrise and sunset,
And on every tenth day, the king of days, I will come
    for the benefit of Tibet.
My future followers who have not met me,
Perform as many prostrations and offerings as you can
To all supports of body, speech, and mind, and in all
    places of accomplishment.
Exert yourselves in accomplishment!
Serve the noble sangha.
This is no different than offerings made to
    Padmasambhava of Uddiyana.
My compassion will never be idle.
I will always help and protect my Tibetan subjects."

The king and his subjects wept in desperation.
Utterly dismayed, they wailed and keened.
All the men and women of Tibet assembled.
They placed the Mahaguru's lotus feet on their heads.
They offered him everything they had.

Mutik Tsenpo, with his ministers, queens, and court,
Offered a kingdom's worth of gold, silver, jewels,
Various soft fabrics, and other fine things.

The Guru said, "Lord and subjects of Tibet, listen!
Freedom and resources are as hard to find as an udumvara.
Human life is as impermanent as winter sunlight.
Samsaric suffering is inexhaustible.
So practice virtue, and benefit will increase.
The results of whatever right and wrong you do in this life
Will be experienced later. They will not disappear.
Therefore focus your mind one-pointedly on dharma.
Carry a qualified guru on the top of your head.
Go for refuge; generate bodhichitta;
And practice the meditation and mantra that purify,
The mandala of accumulation, and guruyoga.
Receive the four empowerments and mix your mind
    with mine.
Foster the point of great liberation upon arising, beyond
    the intellect,
Until you achieve the result, the spontaneously present
    four bodies."
He gave those and many other instructions.

From *An Ornamental Garland of Vajras: A Biography of the
Guru*, the ninth chapter: "The Completion of His Benefit for
Beings in Tibet, and the Preparations for His Departure."

Chapter Ten

His Departure and Subduing of the Rakshasas in the Southwest

Then the king and all his subjects escorted the Guru
To the place of departure for the rakshasa land.
They brought him to the pass at Mangyul Gongthang.
There the master and his company stayed for three days.
He gave individual dharma instruction to each person—
To the king, the subjects, and their attendants.

Then the dakini Yeshe Tsogyal
Offered a precious mandala of gold and turquoise, and said,
"Guru Rinpoche, you know all within the three times.
When you depart from Tibet for the rakshasa land,
Don't leave this woman, Yeshe Tsogyal, behind!
Hold me in your compassion!"

Guru Padma answered,
"You couldn't reach the rakshasa land in this body.
For a time, continue to benefit beings in Tibet.

We are inseparable, and will meet in the ranks of
   vidyadharas."
In that way he did not give his permission for me to leave,
And I remain to benefit beings.[35]

Then the Guru bound the hook mudra and said,
"DZAH HUM BAM HO HUM HUM DZAH HUM."
The four great kings appeared from the clouds,
Leading a steed that they brought before the Guru.

A woman who was, it is said, Princess Mandarava
Appeared amidst rainbow light holding a vase of amrita.
She came before the master and dissolved into his
   khatvanga.[36]
Guru Rinpoche mounted his steed.
The four great kings supported its four legs.[37]
They flew into the southwestern sky.

The Guru ejected the rakshasa king and assumed his
   identity.
He established the whole kingdom in authentic dharma.
Benefit for beings and the teachings continues to increase.

From *An Ornamental Garland of Vajras: A Biography of the
Guru*, the tenth chapter: "His Departure and Subduing of
the Rakshasas in the Southwest."

SAMAYA! Sealed! Sealed! Sealed!

This biography was transcribed by me, Yeshe Tsogyal, in the dakinis' symbol script and concealed as treasure. In the future may it be found by someone with karma! Having been found, may it increase benefit for beings!

SAMAYA! Seal of body! Seal of speech! Seal of mind!

TSATRILAGUHYA!

This was received as siddhi by Padma Garwang Chime Tennyi Lingpa.[38]

Notes

1. Although the biography begins with Guru Rinpoche speaking in the first person, the majority of it is written in the third person. At the end, Yeshe Tsogyal writes in the first person. It is therefore implied that the biography was dictated by Guru Rinpoche to Yeshe Tsogyal and completed by her.

2. "Eightfold waters" are waters with the eight qualities of being sweet, soft, cool, soothing to the throat, free of impurities, free of anything harmful, soothing to the stomach, and refreshing.

3. An udumvara is a type of lotus that blooms once every hundred years.

4. It is generally taught in the treasure tradition that Guru Rinpoche appeared eight, twelve, or twenty-four years after Buddha Shakyamuni's parinirvana.

5. *Danapala* means "protector of generosity."

6. "Yogic conduct" refers, in this case, to behavior that goes against social norms.

7. Maras are demons that attempt to prevent awakening. The term mara can refer either to those forces or tendencies within a person that obstruct their own awakening, or to a person, human or not, who attempts to obstruct the awakening of another. The word can also mean "death," and can therefore also be used to refer to obstructors of one's well-being in general.

8. *Shitavana* means "cool grove."

9. Matrikas are female beings of various types, associated with rage and disturbances. They can be either awakened or mundane. In either case their appearance is said to be threatening. The word *matrika* can be understood to mean "mother," "grandmother," or "matriarch." Dakinis are female beings with magical power, either the supreme magical power of awakening or mundane magical power. Both terms can also be used to refer to emptiness.

10. Throughout this biography the concepts of union and liberation constantly recur. Literally understood, these can refer to sexual union and the liberation of someone's consciousness from samsara. In addition they bear the hidden meaning of two aspects of meditation training: nonduality and liberation upon arising. Guru Rinpoche's "union with the dakinis" can be understood to be the achievement of a state where there is no longer any division of appearances into self and other or into an experiencing cognition and experienced objects. His "liberation of all the males" (sometimes even called "killing all the males") can be understood to mean the achievement of a state where any thought that arises is self-liberated, in that an awareness that recognizes the thought's nature always arises simultaneously with the thought itself.

    In such contexts, *females* can refer to experienced appearances, and *males* to thoughts. Nevertheless the more obvious meaning, Guru Rinpoche's subduing of female spirits through seduction and of male spirits through the liberation of their consciousnesses, is also the text's intention.

11. This chapter begins a section of the biography that records

Guru Rinpoche's accomplishment of eight yidams, collectively called "the eight dispensations." These deities, still practiced today, are the principal yidams of Guru Rinpoche's treasure tradition. In other biographies there are accounts of his receiving instruction on these deities from eight masters, known as "the eight vidyadharas." In this biography his practice of them is correlated with the eight great charnel grounds of central India. In addition, as he accomplishes each of the eight mandalas, he receives a name from the deities. Although these names are not the better-known "eight names of the Guru," their significance is similar.

The eight charnel grounds are often used to represent the eight consciousnesses. The inhabitants of the charnel grounds—the dakinis and the male spirits—can represent the objects of, and the bewilderment associated with, the respective consciousnesses.

"The accomplishment of the eight mandalas" refers, therefore, to the discovery of the wisdoms hidden within the eight consciousnesses. The ensuing union and liberation represent the transcendence of objectification and conceptualization. Thus one can understand this part of the biography as a depiction of Guru Rinpoche's transformation of the eight consciousnesses into the five wisdoms.

Nevertheless he is said to have actually meditated on these deities in the charnel grounds, and to have benefited countless spirits while doing so. Both the literal meaning and the hidden meaning convey aspects of Guru Rinpoche's attainment and activity.

Guna means "qualities," so *Padmagunasambhava* means "lotus-born with qualities."

12. The supreme siddhi is the attainment of awakening. Common siddhis are such things as supercognition (extrasensory perception) and magical power.

13. *Samyak* means "authentic" or "perfect." Here it refers to the deity Authentic Heruka.

14. These are articles of jewelry made from human bone, ointment

made from human ashes, and garments of tiger skin, elephant skin, and human skin. The purpose of wearing such apparently grisly things is threefold: to remind the yogin of impermanence and death, to point out emptiness as the nature of all things, and to indicate the equality of samsara and nirvana. Since these are also the three purposes of remaining in charnel grounds, those who did so customarily wore these adornments.

15. "Direct action" is the liberation from samsara of a being's consciousness. For this to be done, there must be a karmic connection, either positive or negative, between the liberating buddha or bodhisattva and the liberated being. The *Yamantaka Tantra* teaches twelve activities associated with this.

16. Because Yamantaka is the wrathful form of Manjushri, the embodiment of the prajna of all buddhas, Guru Rinpoche received this name.

17. Vajrakumara, which means "vajra youth," is another name for the deity Vajrakila, who embodies the activity or karmas of all buddhas.

18. "The four actions" are pacification, increase, attraction, and force.

19. Tobden Nakpo, the Powerful Black One, is the principal deity in the mandala of Forceful Mantra.

20. For the sake of clarity, I have capitalized the word guru when it refers to Guru Rinpoche and reads *gu.ru.* in the Tibetan, but have left it uncapitalized when it is used generically and translates *bla.ma.* in the Tibetan.

21. "The five sciences" are linguistics, construction and art, medicine, logic, and dharma.

22. "The wisdoms of the four joys" are stages in the sequence of the mind entering a state where all disturbance and bewilderment are, at least temporarily, in abeyance. The first three of these

are mundane; the fourth has both mundane and supra mundane varieties.

23. A *vidyadhara* is a "holder of awareness," either the supramundane awareness of the nature of things, or mundane magical or scientific knowledge. In tantra the term can refer either to any empowered practitioner or to an attained practitioner. In the second case there are said to be four types of vidyadharas, who are distinguished by their degree of attainment. A "vidyadhara of full ripening" has transformed his or her mind, but not his or her body (the full ripening of previous karma), into a deity. A "vidyadhara with mastery over life" has in addition gained control over the duration of his or her life. A "vidyadhara of Mahamudra" has transformed his or her form into the great seal (Mahamudra) of a deity's form. A "vidyadhara of spontaneous presence" has achieved perfect awakening.

24. Guru Rinpoche and Mandarava.

25. The term *tirthika* refers to adherents of non-Buddhist Indian religions. It was translated into Tibetan as *mu.steg.pa.*, which can be understood to mean "forders" in the metaphoric sense of those who are at least attempting to cross the ocean of samsara. It is therefore understood in the Tibetan tradition to be far from pejorative.

However, since the places of ritual ablution used by Hindus were called *tirtha*, "shallow places in a river where it might be forded or where one might wash," it seems possible that it originally meant "those who go to fords" to perform ritual ablution. It could still, of course, be rendered "forders" in English.

26. "The eight types of haughty beings," sometimes called "the eight classes of gods and spirits," are devas, nagas, asuras, yamas, matrikas, yakshas, rakshasas, and bhutas. They are all nonhuman, powerful mundane beings.

27. Nine spirits with great influence over Tibet.

28. The Glorious Copper-Colored Mountain is Guru Rinpoche's nirmanakaya pure realm.

29. The Tiger Year referred to must be either 858 or 918 C.E. and the Horse Year either 862 or 922 C.E. Although each of the sixty-year cycles of the Tibetan calendar has a name and number, the first numbered cycle did not begin until 1027. The dating of events before then is therefore less precise.

30. Bön is the indigenous religion of Tibet. According to Buddhist sources, present-day Bön is what is called in this text "the tradition with the authentic view."

31. "Dictates" are what the Buddha taught; "shastras" are commentaries on them.

32. This is an elaborate mandala that includes twenty-one mandalas within it, such as those of the eight dispensations and others. The best-known treasures concerned with this are those of Guru Chöwang and Chokgyur Dechen Lingpa.

33. *Ganachakra* means "gathering circle" and is the term for a tantric feast.

34. Rakshasas are said to be corporeal nonhumans who eat human beings.

35. By speaking here in the first person, Yeshe Tsogyal identifies herself as the writer.

36. A staff, sometimes used to represent a consort.

37. The four rulers of the lowest of the deva realms. They are protectors of dharma.

38. The name used by Jamgön Lodrö Taye as a revealer of treasure.

Vairochana, the Great Emanated Translator

The Lotus Garden

A Biography of Vairochana, the Great Emanated Translator

Chapter One

The Birth of Vairochana

EMAHO!
To all the victorious sugatas
Of all places and times, and your children;
To the excellent teacher,
The peerless victor of the Shakyas;
To the best of places,
Jambudvipa's Vajrasana in India;
To the retinue of shravakas and bodhisattvas;
To the holy dharma;
And to that time:
To fivefold excellence[1]
I bow from my heart with undivided faith.

To the master of the Great Perfection teachings,
    Shri Singha;
To immortal Padmasambhava,
Whose splendor overpowers all that appears and exists;

The Lotus Garden

To Vimala,
The crown ornament of all the learned and accomplished;
To Shantarakshita,
The holder of the vinayapitaka;
And to King Trisong,
The root of the teachings in the Himalayas:
To those of peerless kindness, I pay homage.

At the great offering on the tenth day of the
    waxing moon[2]
In the middle month of autumn
In the Female Water Sheep Year[3]
Vairochana was accompanied by the three fortunate
    Khampas:[4]
Yudra Nyingpo, Doksher Nakpo, and Mipam Gönpo.
Hundreds of those with karma were also assembled there.
Gathered like clouds, they placed Vairochana's feet on
    their heads.

Then the dharmaraja Doksher Nakpo offered
To the great learned translator Vairochana
Beautiful garments, delicious drinks,
And a precious mandala of gold and turquoise,
And said, "Vairochana, our guide:
I have a past store of karmic residue and merit.
I met you,
The master who knows all within the three times.
I encountered the resultant dharma,
Authentic secret mantra.
I have practiced it to the point
Where I will die free of regret.

I request that you,
The great treasury of kind and excellent compassion,
Speak of the essence of your life and deeds."

Vairochana answered,
"Your Majesty and my other two fortunate disciples, listen!
Although my life is inconceivable,
I will describe it to this assembly.
Hold it in your minds!

"In the past, in the divine land of India,
I was Ananda, Shakyamuni's attendant.
He was the best of arhats,
An emanation of the buddha Vairochana.[5]
He passed into nirvana, and became me.

"The way in which I was emanated in this world
In order to light the beacon of authentic dharma
In this dark land of Tibet was thus:
The expanse of dharmakaya is the clear light
That equally pervades samsara and nirvana.

"It has always been permanent, stable, manifest wisdom.
However, in order to guide beings through appropriate
   emanations,
It emanated a human body with the eight freedoms.[6]
During the first eight years of my life I gradually acquired
The ten excellent resources.

"I was not born into an arrogant royal family.
My father was Pagor Hedö, of good descent.

The Lotus Garden

My mother was Drenka Zadrön.
I was born to them on the tenth day
Of the last summer month in the Ox Year,[7]
A Thursday, under the constellation Victory,
At sunrise, the Hour of the Dragon.

"The sky was filled with rainbow clouds and a rain
   of flowers.
The earth shook and the air roared with thunder.
Everyone in that area was amazed.
They all assembled and asked one another what
   was happening.

"In that land was a rishi called Lekpay Lodrö,[8]
A self-arisen siddha who saw the truth.
The people decided to ask him what was occurring.
Birana, Tsewang Namka, Sönam Özer, and Dawa Zangpo
Were dispatched as fast-running messengers.

"They saw a five-colored rainbow appearing from the west
Above the residence of Pagor Hedö.
It started from the west.
It ended in the east.
Again all the people discussed this
And went to Pagor Hedö's home.

"I, the emanation of the buddha Vairochana,
Had been born to Drenza Metok Palgyi Drönma.
I possessed all the good signs of superiority.

"Immediately after my birth I recited,

'NAMO BUDDHA DHARMA SANGHAYA.
I bow to the buddha, dharma, and sangha.
I will perform the beneficial deeds of a bodhisattva.
May the beacon of dharma be lit in this dark land.'

"When I said this, it was heard by all gathered there.
They remembered it and later repeated it to others.
At the same time they heard
Many gods and goddesses playing music
And saw them wash me with amrita.

"There was a pleasant fragrance and a gentle, cool rain.
My black hair and white teeth shone.
I smiled tranquilly.
My eyes were long and my nose high-bridged.

"I was as handsome as a child of the gods.
Merely seeing me caused faith and devotion.
All delighted in me and prayed to me.
After the four runners had arrived there,
They gently addressed the whole gathering.

" 'We four asked the rishi Lekpay Lodrö about these signs.
He answered well with words of truth.
"Such signs have never been seen," he said,
"Nor will they be seen again.
Their meaning is unknown to me.
We must ask the gods."

" 'He entered into meditation and struck the ground
   with his palm.

He proclaimed the power of true words.
The earth shook.
In front of the rishi appeared the goddess of the earth,
    who cried,
"What is wrong that you invoke the power of true
    words in such a way?"

" 'The rishi replied, "Goddess of the earth,
I compelled you because I do not understand
These excellent signs, previously unknown.
Please explain their meaning."

"""Great rishi, tormentor of gods," she said,
"From the realm of Highest Dense Array above,
An emanation of Buddha Vairochana has appeared
    in human form.
He is Ananda, Shakyamuni's attendant, passed into
    another life,
And has now been born as Pagor Hedö's son.

"""The sky filled with rainbow clouds is a sign
That he is blessed as the son of all victorious sugatas.
The rain of multicolored flowers is a sign
That he is acclaimed by all gods.

"""The appearance from the west of a five-colored rainbow
Above the house of Pagor Hedö is a sign
That this supreme nirmanakaya
Has come from Tibet in the west.

"""The rainbow pointing back to Tibet is a sign

That he will not remain here but go there.
The white end of the rainbow planted in the east
Is a sign that his supreme field of activity
For disciples will be in Tsawarong in the east.

"""It is a sign that he will make it a place of virtue
With the dharma of absolute truth.
A LA LA LA HO
A buddha has come to this world!
SIDDHI PHALA!
The supreme dharma has come!
SANGHA JNANA!
The noble sangha has come!"[9]

" 'Saying that, the goddess disappeared.
Then the rishi Lekpay Lodrö said,
"Go quickly and tell those gathered there!"
So we four have come here.'

"Delighted, all the people from the area went to
      their homes
And then returned with much wealth,
Which they offered to us, mother, father, and son.
I remained there until I was eight."[10]

From *The Lotus Garden, A Biography of Vairochana*, the first
chapter: "The Birth of Vairochana."

Chapter Two

His Acceptance by Manjushri and Receiving of the Empowerment of Awareness-Display

That boy grew more quickly than others,
Each year, month, and day.
He was superior to and unlike all others.
Everyone in the area was amazed.

In his third year, the Year of the Hare,[11]
He went to see the rishi Lekpay Lodrö,
Who taught him the dharma
Of pratyekabuddhas who've seen the truth.

Through mere introduction, the boy understood it all.
He came to be known as Genjak Thangta.
One day he went to gather flowers
And fell asleep.

He dreamed that two beautiful goddesses appeared,
Washed him with amrita,

And gave him much food and drink.

They said to him,
"Go to a place one yojana from here,[12]
Where there is a white boulder like piled jewels.
You will find there a great, secret gathering cave of
    the dakinis.
Enter it and its occupant will appear."

He awoke and remembered his dream.
His whole body was filled with bliss and his
    belly was full.
Wondering if such a place existed, he went to look.
A white rainbow coming from the southeast
Ended at the place spoken of.
He went there and found it to be as in his dream.

Entering the cave,
He found an old man inside it,
Who exclaimed, "My son has come!"
And clapped his hands.

Genjak was terrified and said,
"I am not your son; I am my father's son!
I will not stay here. I must go!"
The old man grabbed Genjak's clothing with
    his left hand,
And said, "TRI RAM HUM! TRI RAM HUM!"

With his right hand
He pointed a sharp sword at the little boy's heart,

And said, "AVARANA PRAVESHAYA PHAT!
JNANA PRAJNA AVESHAYA HO!"[13]
As he said this, he melted into light
And in an instant appeared clearly as Manjushri.

Then the two goddesses from the dream, delighted,
Said to the boy, "Genjak Thangta, this is Manjushri.
Pay respectful homage and request empowerment now!"

He replied, "I don't know how to pay homage,
Nor how to request empowerment."

"Then we can show you," they said. "Do this."
The goddesses requested empowerment.

He imitated them, saying,
"I know how to request empowerment!"

From the syllables of Manjushri's body, speech,
    and mind
Radiated rays of light, white, red, and blue.
They dissolved into Genjak Thangta's three gates
    of the senses.
Manjushri's form was withdrawn into a mass
    of light,
Which became mixed with Genjak's mind.

His awareness became lucid and vivid.
When he came to himself,
None of those appearances were there.
He was thereafter able to understand all mundane things

Upon simply being shown them.
His discernment was supreme, greater than before.
He went home and told his parents of all this.
Amazed, they said, "Tell no one!"

From *The Lotus Garden, A Biography of Vairochana*, the second chapter: "His Acceptance by Manjushri and Receiving of the Empowerment of Awareness-Display."

Chapter Three

His Display of Miracles

In his fifth year he accompanied his father
On a journey to worship the local deities.
On the way they were given abundant meat and drink
By a merchant called Argö, who said,
"Give me your young son, Genjak Thangta.
I will pay you anything you ask,
Even my wives, my servants, and all I own!
I have no son and want yours.
Many have offered me their sons,
But yours is vastly superior
In beauty and intelligence.
Give me your son and I will protect you both
From all suffering!"

In response, Pagor Hedö said,
"If I had any other sons, I would give you this one,
But he is an only child without siblings.

If we have more children in the future
I will give him to you then."

The merchant cried, "Oh, don't say that!" and fled.
Continuing their journey, they reached a forested valley.
Within it was a field of flowers of many colors.
Pagor Hedö went to perform a lhasang.[14]

Genjak Thangta lay down.
A monkey gathered various delicious fruits
And offered them to the boy.
Then the monkey and boy played together happily.

His father saw this and felt faith in his son, thinking,
"If he were anyone else, the monkey would flee in fear.
This monkey likes Genjak Thangta and plays with him,
And has brought him lots of delicious fruit.
This boy is better than others."

When he approached his son, the monkey fled.
Genjak Thangta offered the fruit to his father,
Who ate a little of it and brought most of it home.
Telling Drenkaza the story, he gave her the fruit.[15]
Amazed, she praised her son.

On one occasion, Genjak Thangta went to view
A great public gathering.
On the way he came upon a rabbit that was lying
    unconscious.
He threw a stone at it, killing it.
Drenka Zadrön saw this and said,

"Son, from infancy until now you have never
    harmed others.
You have always gotten along with everyone.
In killing this innocent being you have done great evil.
Don't return home!"

Genjak Thangta thought, "My mother is right.
Although it was not my intention to kill it,
Although I meant no harm, it died through karma.
What should I do?"

Very afraid, he answered his mother,
"Mother, don't say that! Listen to your son!
I meant no harm with this stone.
A little pebble shouldn't have killed a rabbit.
Nevertheless through karma I have killed.
If I, Genjak Thangta, had no intention to kill,
If this rabbit died as a result of its own karma,
May that which has died return to life at this instant!"

Through his forceful aspiration
The rabbit returned to life and ran off into the hills.
The boy's mother was delighted.
The assembled crowd was amazed.
They praised Genjak Thangta and aspired to emulate him.

From *The Lotus Garden, A Biography of Vairochana*, the third
chapter: "His Display of Miracles."

Chapter Four

His Journey to Central Tibet

In the eighth year of his life
The many children of his area gathered to cut bamboo.
They carried wooden bows and arrows
And competed in archery,
Aiming at a target of piled earth and stones.
Genjak Thangta surpassed all the others.

On another occasion,
Pagor Hedö and Drenka Zadrön
Went to a marketplace where many were gathered.
At mid-morning the king, Trisong Detsen, arrived
    at their home
Accompanied by many servants.
He summoned Genjak Thangta, who came before him.

The king said, "Little boy, where do you live?
What are your parents called? What is your name?

Answer me well!"

The boy answered the king's questions truthfully,
Saying, "My father is Pagor Hedö.
My mother is called Drenka Zadrön.
I am called Genjak Thangta.
This is my home."
He pointed to the entrance.
The king, amazed, presented the boy
With a beverage made of seven fine foods.

Then he said to his ministers,
"Padmasambhava, the master from Uddiyana,
Predicted a translator. It is this boy!"
To the minister, Bami Trisher,
The king said, "Talk to him!"

The minister asked, "Little boy, are your parents within?
Have they gone out? Where have they gone?"

The boy answered, "My father has gone to market
    to buy meat.
My mother has gone to buy sesame oil.
Three days from now we must celebrate the New Year."

The king exclaimed, "Son, why do you remain here?
You must come with me. Get ready!"

The boy replied, "If my parents give their permission,
I will ride behind you on your horse."

The king asked, "Do you know how to translate
  holy dharma?"

"Not at present, but I will if taught", the boy replied.

The king asked, "Can you bear a long journey?"

"I can bear going anywhere with my parents' permission,"
The boy replied.
The king was pleased; the connection was made.

The king said, "Take the boy ahead.
I will stay behind to talk to his parents.
After I have paid them his price, I'll catch up with you."

But Genjak Thangta interjected,
"I dare not go until I ask my parents!
Wait! They will arrive presently."

The king said, "He's right," and waited.
Pagor Hedö appeared bearing meat and liquor.
Then Drenza Drönkyi appeared bearing sesame oil.[16]

The king asked, "Little boy, are these your parents?"

The boy replied, "They are."

Pleased, the king said,
"Pagor Hedö, come here!"
Delighted, he did so.

He placed the king's feet on his head and asked,
"For what service has Your Majesty come here?"

The king replied, "Good Pagor Hedö,
I have no reason to be here
Other than your young son, Genjak Thangta.
There is much holy dharma in India.
I have come here
So that it may be translated and brought to Tibet.
The vidyadhara and master Padmasambhava
Has said that this cannot happen without your son.
It is the command of the victors,
The proven prophecy of the noble ones!
Give him to me and I will pay you whatever you wish."

Pagor Hedö became terrified and said,
"Great dharma king, please don't say this!
This boy is the only loved one of his parents.
Who could bear to send him to another land?
He is only an eight-year-old boy!
How could he get to India?
He doesn't even know how to talk!
He is dull and unintelligent.
How could he ever learn to translate from Sanskrit?
We, his parents, are old.
We have no other children.
On whom would we depend?
Even if you kill me, I will not offer him to you.
Your Majesty, please give this up!"

The king replied,

"Pagor Hedö, don't say that!
Although your son is young now,
He won't be sent until he is grown.
He may seem dull and unintelligent,
But Guru Rinpoche is never wrong!
His intelligence will increase with each month and year.
It is true that you two have no other child to love,
But I will take responsibility for your happiness."

He forcefully placed the boy on a horse
And sent him ahead, surrounded by twenty runners.
He gave Pagor Hedö and his wife a thousand ingots of
gold and of silver,
A hundred horses, a hundred mules, a hundred dzos,
a hundred dris,
Tea, a thousand bolts of silk, and a thousand bolts
of cotton.

He assured them, saying, "Don't be sad!
Follow your son and settle near him!
I will treat him with love and kindness."

So the parents went along
And settled in Yarlung Zowathang.
Genjak Thangta went to the upper story
Of the central temple at Samye.

From *The Lotus Garden, A Biography of Vairochana*, the fourth
chapter: "His Journey to Central Tibet."

Chapter Five

The Meeting of Genjak Thangta with the Abbot, the Master, and the Dharma King, and His Translation of Dharma

Then the dharma king Trisong Detsen
Requested the master Padmasambhava
To be seated on a throne of gold
In the great central temple at Samye.
The great abbot Shantarakshita
Was seated on a throne of silver.
Genjak Thangta was seated on three piled cushions.

The king offered a mandala
Of gold, silver, turquoise, and coral.
He requested the teaching of holy dharma in Tibet.
The great master gave the awareness-entrustment
    of Manjushri.
Genjak Thangta understood its meaning.
The bodhisattva taught medicine.
Genjak Thangta also understood this completely.

Then, at the beginning of his training as a translator,
He translated into Tibetan
The *Tantra of the Magical Net of Manjushri*,
The *Tantra of the Single Magic of the Essence of Wisdom*,
A Summary of Secret Mantra's Path of Means,
   and other texts.

He came to understand translation,
And became known as Vairochana.[17]
He lived in the upper story of Samye's
Central temple for seven years.
Trisong Detsen treated him like his own son.

From *The Lotus Garden, A Biography of Vairochana*, the fifth
chapter: "The Meeting of Genjak Thangta with the Abbot,
the Master, and the Dharma King, and His Translation of
Dharma."

Chapter Six

The Concealment of Water by the Two Lake Goddesses, Vairochana's Placement of Them Under Samaya, and His Achievement of Siddhi

Then the abbot, master, and dharma king,
Accompanied by Vairochana, the queen, and the ministers,
Went to the peak of Mount Hepo near Samye.
They performed an elaborate ganachakra.

At that time Guru Padma said,
"Your Majesty and all you others, please listen!
It is inappropriate to teach dharma
Based solely on one's own authority.
In order that you resolve any doubts about the dharma
That the great abbot and I have translated,
Send Vairochana and others who know translation
    to India."

The abbot said, "Good!"
The dharma king said,
"I am one-pointedly devoted

To both the abbot and the master.
I therefore have no doubts to resolve.
Vairochana is like my only son, and is young.
If he were sent to India
For the sole purpose of translation,
It would be difficult for him to reach his destination.
I therefore request that for the time being
The abbot and master continue to teach
Profound, authentic holy dharma."

The bodhisattva replied,
"Great dharma king, listen to me well!
For the sake of the confidence of those other than you,
Send this boy to Vajrasana in India!
Cause the dual doctrine of sutra and mantra
To be translated into Tibetan!
Establish this great kingdom in holy dharma!
Vairochana's journey will be without impediment.
He will bring back much
Extremely profound, superior holy dharma."

The king was pleased by what the abbot said,
And prepared to send Vairochana
And Tsangngon Lekdrup to India,
Accompanied by two servants.

The king provided each of the two translators
With fifty-one measures of gold powder
And seven thousand silver ingots.
The abbot, master, and dharma king
Saw them off, praying for them.

On the way, Vairochana thought,
"If my previous aspirations are powerful,
I will be able to reach India.
If I have accumulated good habits,
It is even possible that I might retrieve authentic
    holy dharma.
If there is a powerful karmic momentum,
It is even possible that I might meet Indian pandits.
If the dharma I have learned up to now is true,
May my wishes be accomplished in accord with dharma!"

With that aspiration he went to India.
When they reached the border of Tibet and Nepal,
They searched for water for tea but found none.
The place was dark and empty, without habitation.

Lekdrup said, "Let us go no farther. We'll sleep here.
Tomorrow morning we'll find water."
Saying that, he lay down in a lotus garden.

Vairochana said,
"There is a saying common to India and Tibet:
If fellow travelers on a long journey disagree,
It is like the meeting of a raven and an owl in the north.
Don't be quarrelsome! Whatever you say is fine."
Vairochana looked and saw at a distance of
    two bowshots
A blazing fire producing a lot of smoke.

He said, "Lekdrup and my other companions, listen!
Not far from here, along our way, a fire is burning.

Let's see what it is!"
The two servants agreed to get up and look.

Lekdrup said, "It must be a band of merchants.
If we wander over there at night,
We'll be eaten alive by their dogs.
Don't talk so loudly! Lie back down in silence!"

Vairochana wanted to see what it was.
He untied his meditation belt and went there stealthily.[18]
As he got closer, the fire seemed to shrink and the
    light to increase.
He thought, "I should flee, and return to our
    campsite.
I didn't listen to Lekdrup when he told me to stay put.
Still, I will not flee! Thoughts are demons!
If I mistake my mind for a demon,
I am not Vairochana!"

He wrote down that thought
And then rested evenly for a while
In the expanse of dharmata.
Then he looked again and saw a ball of light,
Its radiance filling the whole lotus garden.
Approaching the light, he found two large fish
Flopping about on the dry land.

Vairochana thought, "This is strange!
There is no water in this place.
It is impossible for these fish to have come here!
It's hard to tell whether this is good or bad.

It could be an impediment to my search
For authentic, profound holy dharma.
I should meditate."

He rested in the samadhi
Of the awareness mantra of Vajradhara,
And pointed his staff at the fishes' bellies.
He realized that they were two sister lake goddesses.
Vairochana sang this song of fourfold fearlessness:

"I, Vairochana of the view
Of primordially pure wisdom,
Am unafraid of the dense habits
Of ignorance and bewilderment,
Of dualistic thoughts of gods and demons,
And of the narrow passage
Between permanence and termination.[19]

"For me, Vairochana of self-liberating meditation,
The generation stage is appearance-emptiness,
A water-moon dance of deities' forms.[20]
It is without the flaw of substantial form and
    characteristics.
I am unafraid of the narrow passage
Between the hallucinations of dualistic appearances.

"I, Vairochana, hold the mastery of disciplined conduct.
I am without hope, fear, joy, and suffering.
Even if the threefold world were destroyed,[21]
The wisdom vajra would be beyond birth and death.
I am unafraid of others.

"I, Vairochana of the result,
  The spontaneously present four bodies-
  The dharmakaya, utterly pure nature;
  The self-illuminating sambhogakaya;
  And compassion, the nirmanakaya-
  Am unafraid of anyone.
  Samsara and nirvana are primordially liberated.

"You two sister lake goddesses,
  Mental embodiments of bewildered thought,
  Cause no obstacles!
  Obey my commands and samaya![22]
  Since this beggar, Vairochana,
  Has no wealth to bring to India,
  He requests siddhi of you."

Then he forcefully exclaimed, "Hum!"
  The lake goddesses were terrified
  And turned from fish into dragons.
  They flew into the sky and gave a tremendous roar.

Vairochana transformed himself into two lions,
  Their eyes wide with rage.
  The two dragons fell to the ground
  And turned into two beautiful girls.

They said, "Vairochana,
  Great holder of awareness mantra,
  If you search for holy dharma,
  We would not dare to obstruct you.
  Let us go!

We will serve you however you wish."

They then offered a begging bowl filled with gold powder,
Along with their life essences.
They gave their promise and bond.[23]
Vairochana looked and saw that the whole area
Was filled with lakes and rivers.

Since on the previous day there had been no sign
  of water there,
And on that day the place was one swirling lake,
It was certain that the lake goddesses had concealed
  the water.
He wondered where Lekdrup and his other
  companions were.

Looking for them, he found them in the lotus garden,
Which was now surrounded by water.
They were amazed.

Vairochana told them the story,
And showed them the begging bowl filled with gold.
They were delighted and even more amazed.

From *The Lotus Garden, A Biography of Vairochana*, the sixth
chapter: "The Concealment of Water by the Two Lake Goddesses, Vairochana's Placement of Them Under Samaya, and
His Achievement of Siddhi."

Chapter Seven

His Translation of Dharma in India

Thirty-five days after that
They reached the border of India and Nepal.
They came to a great forest.
An atsara appeared,[24]
Running toward them at great speed.

He held in his hands three dice,
And said to them,
"DHARVISULA ARSINGNAYA!"[25]
They didn't understand him,
But accompanied him anyway.

After a while they came to a lotus garden.
Vairochana fell asleep
And dreamed of an iron she-wolf
Who said she was the glorious Protectress of Mantra.[26]

Fire blazing from her mouth, she was terrifying.
She said, "You foolish, deceived monk from Tibet!
If you seek authentic dharma,
Why are you accompanying this atsara?
This land is an island of rakshasas,
A place where anyone who appears is eaten alive!

"The valley to the right is the region of Nepal called
    Shuphu.
If you go there, you will discover a way to India
And the holy dharma of the nine vehicles,[27]
Which correspond to the best, intermediate,
And least faculties among individuals.

"The pandits who teach them are like that as well.
The best dharma accords with the best faculties:
Mahayoga, anu, ati, chiti, yangti, and the complete
    great end.[28]
The best pandits and siddhas are the vidyadhara
    Shri Singha;
The great master from Uddiyana, Padmasambhava;
And the mahapandit from Kashmir, Vimalamitra.
They are learned in the Great Perfection, the
    spontaneous peak.
Therefore, son, rely upon those three as teachers.

As well, receive much instruction
From all the learned and accomplished of India
Without making distinction in quality.
The victors teach nothing useless.
Therefore learn all you can.

Indian patrons of the teachings may resent you
Because of their love for dharma,
So don't say that you are translating dharma;
Keep it secret.
I will always protect you."

Saying that, she flew into space and disappeared.
When he awoke he told his companions of his dream.
They agreed to follow her advice,
And went to the valley on the right.

They found their way to India, the land of the noble.
They asked what learned mahapandits there were,
And were told that among
The five hundred mahapandits attending the king,
Vimalamitra, Mahahumkara, and Shakyanila
    were the best.

It was said that their equal did not exist
On the earth or under the sun.
They went on and asked a potter, who said,
"The mahavidyadhara Shri Singha has no equal.
After him is Vimalamitra.
The others are also all learned and accomplished,
For if an ordinary person were to teach in a
    dharma college,
The king would punish him.
Therefore whoever they are, they are learned."

Vairochana then went to meet the mahapandit
    Vimalamitra,

One of five hundred chaplains of the king.
Vairochana couldn't understand his speech,
But felt devotion for his form.

Vairochana offered Vimalamitra
Three measures of gold dust, a golden bowl,
And a palm leaf on which was written:
"DHARMA JNANA SIDDHI PHALA HO!
GURU RATNA ATI PASHAM HUM!"[29]

Vimala read this, laughed, and clapped his hands.
He replied, "DHARMA PRAJNA JNANA SIDDHI BHRUM!
A LA LA HO KAMA DANA HI!"

Translated, this means:
"Discernment and wisdom of dharma,
Treasury of attainment; wondrous!
If you want it, I can give it!"

Vairochana understood, and waited.
Vimalamitra then said, "Come here.
What is your name? What is your caste?
Do you know Padmasambhava of Uddiyana?
Where is Shantarakshita, the abbot from Zahor?
What dharma is he teaching?"

Vairochana replied, "My name is Vairochana.
My caste is of the commoners.
My liege lord is Trisong Detsen,
An emanation of Manjushri and the king of Tibet.
At present both Padmasambhava of Uddiyana

And Shantarakshita are in Tibet;
They are my gurus.
They are teaching much profound dharma
Of outer and inner secret mantra.
I am their translator.
In order to resolve my doubts,
I have been sent here by the abbot, master, and king.
Please look kindly upon me!
I beg of you, please teach
The profound, authentic dharma of absolute truth!"

To this Vimalamitra replied,
"If you are of sharp faculties,
The earth is covered with dharma.
If you are a vessel,
The dharma of secret mantra exists.
Tibetan monk, Vairochana,
You must have gathered accumulations
In previous lives to have met me in this one.
First learn the pratimoksha, vinaya, and sutras,
The undisputed and widely known teachings
    of the Buddha.
First translate the sutras. Then learn mantra."

In the beginning, he translated the *Vinayagama,*
    the *Vinayottara,*
The *Sutra on the Deeds of Awakening,*
The *Sutra on the Purification of Lower State,*
The *Jnanagarbhasutra,* the *Amoghapashasutra,*
The *Sutra on Distinguishing Karmas,*
The *Sutra of a Hundred Karmas,*

The *Collected Dictates,*
The *Amoghapashatantra,* and the *Uttaratantra.*
He translated many sutras and tantras,
Medicine and astrology,
Dharma and Bön, and other things.

Then he translated the outer, inner, secret, and very
  secret tantras:
The kriya, charya, yoga, and anuttarayogatantras,
Including the three sections of kriya, upa, and yoga,
The tantras of chiti, yangti, and the spontaneous
  great end,
Various forms of rasayana, and the channels and
  winds of chandali.[30]
He translated them at night, and also practiced them.

He translated the eighteen tantras of the mind class,[31]
The mother and son tantras of the expanse class,
And various texts of the instruction class—
Teachings of the Great Perfection—
As well as various applications of forceful mantra.
He went to many learned pandits and siddhas
For instruction in various sciences and their applications.

From *The Lotus Garden, A Biography of Vairochana*, the seventh chapter: "His Translation of Dharma in India."

Chapter Eight

His Translation of Dharma in India and Preparations for His Return to Tibet

Then the translator Vairochana
Studied under twenty other learned Indians.
Having become learned and having achieved siddhi,
He prepared to return to Tibet.

Vimalamitra gave him some advice from his heart:
"If you wish to translate dharma,
You must be perfect.
So remain here for a while.
You will eventually become learned.
The distance between Tibet and India is great.
It cannot be traversed at just any time.
So relax!"

Vairochana's companion, Lekdrup, said,
"If we don't return to Tibet now,
And we become too learned,

The people of India will not let us go.
Our lives will be in danger!
If we wait too long,
We will suffer our lord's punishment.
I won't stay here!
I'm going home!"

Vairochana replied,
"The command of one's guru is extremely significant.
Wait a while. We'll go together.
No matter how learned we become,
Because there are so many pandits in India,
How could we be noticed?"

Lekdrup didn't listen, and went on ahead.
Vairochana stayed in India
And studied the five subsequent mind-class tantras.
One day three messengers were sent
From the royal palace to summon Vimalamitra.
Vairochana went then to meet Humkara.

He received from him and translated
The *Tantra of the Single Wisdom of the Great Perfection*,
The *Vast Sphere, the Separation of Mind and Awareness*,
The *Outer and Inner Separation of Samsara and Nirvana*,
The *Agama of Ocean Ablution*,
The *Tantra of Ripening Empowerments*,
The mother and son tantras of the expanse class,
And many tantras of the instruction class.

He went to many learned and accomplished mahapandits,

And translated both sutra and mantra,
Outer, inner, and secret dharma.
Especially, from the vidyadhara Shri Singha,
He received all the tantras and empowerments
Of the Great Perfection.

Vairochana achieved supreme learning.
He was happy and at ease.
But by that time all the people of the area
Had become suspicious of him.
They had heard of Tibetan monks coming to India
And carrying authentic holy dharma back to Tibet.
One person talked of this to another
Until it was heard by the queen.
She discussed it with a minister
And they told the king.

He said, "Bring me whoever started the rumors!"
They traced the rumors back to their source,
Using the king's authority to do so.
They found that in a village called Warte
Lived a woman who sold both food and wine.

She told them that a young Tibetan had appeared,
Bought food, and spoken of translation.
Carrying many books, he had gone on his way.
The ministers conferred and sent forth seven runners.
They told them to kill the young Tibetan
And to return with his head and heart.

Lekdrup saw the runners approaching

And hid in the forest.
The runners included an atsara
Who possessed slight supercognition,
With which he searched the area.
"The Tibetan hasn't been here," he said,
"But he will come to the barrier at the border."

They went on for a distance of three yojanas
And lay down in hiding near the barrier.
At nightfall Lekdrup appeared.
They caught and killed him.
They cut off his head and cut out his heart
And presented them to the king.

Unsatisfied, the king conferred with his ministers.
"There may be other Tibetans," he said.
"Send many soldiers and stop them!"
Twenty-five atsaras and many others were sent
To guard the border.
Vairochana heard of this and became frightened.
He asked the pandits what he should do.

He was told, "If you obey your guru's commands,
And use his instructions as your eyes,
You will be protected from all danger
Through the power of his compassion.

"If you don't rely on the guru's instructions,
You become like someone who wishes
To cross the water in a boat
Yet destroys himself and others

Because he fails in skill.

"Anyone who relies on a guru
Yet breaks his commands
Will fall down in the future
And suffer inauspiciousness now.

"Vairochana, understand this!
Place a qualified guru atop your head!
Don the armor of instructions
That bestow fearless bravery!

"Take up the razor-sharp weapons
Of forceful mantra!
Accomplish the siddhi of fleetness of foot,
Which evades all pursuit!

"Wear the cloak of invisibility that is
Like being hidden among trees.
Translate dharma with the faculty
Of perfect recollection.

"Write down whatever you can't remember
And carry it on your back.
Bring along the mother and sister dakinis
And the dharmapalas as bodyguards.

"If you are skilled in archery,
Your arrows are unstoppable.
If you have wings,
It is easy to fly in the sky.

If you possess instructions,
It is impossible for you to be afraid of anyone."
They gave him much advice like this using symbols.

Vairochana replied, "Excellent! I will do all that!"
The pandits and siddhas gave him the instructions.
Vairochana accomplished perfect recollection,
Fleetness of foot, and invisibility.
Through his mastery of those and other instructions
Vairochana achieved fearless confidence
And prepared to set out for Tibet.

From *The Lotus Garden, A Biography of Vairochana*, the eighth chapter: "His Translation of Dharma in India and Preparations for His Return to Tibet."

Chapter Nine

Slander of His Dharma Teaching, and the Averting of Obstacles

Then Vimalamitra, Humkara,
Shri Singha, and other pandits and siddhas
Said to him, "Vairochana, you are unlike others.
We have blessed you as the son of our hearts.
You have now received
All of the most profound instructions.
Keep them secret!

"When you return to Tibet,
Don't teach these instructions right away.
It would cause misunderstandings.
Why? Because this dharma
Does not easily fit into the intellect.
So teach the dharma of the sutras.

"A time will come for the teaching
Of these instructions,

But don't disseminate the essence of profound dharma
In the presence of the unreceptive.
Teach it only to those who earnestly seek it,
And not to those whose faith is just in the mouth.

"Don't exchange instructions and awareness
For illusory wealth and possessions.
Kings rule over everyone,
But they don't rule over dharma.

"Don't break the seal!
If you gain a reputation for learning,
Slander will come from India.
Don't proclaim your reputation!

"Say, 'I don't have it! I don't know!'
Since Tibet is a borderland,
A land of demons,
There will be much doubt.
Obstacles will come!

"However, if you possess instruction,
Wherever you go will be the realm of disciples.
Don't lose your dharma texts!
Always be ready to run!

"Don't forget your gurus!
Always pray from your heart!
If you keep your samaya,
You will be protected by our compassion."
Vairochana offered each of them

A measure of gold powder in gratitude.
Each of his masters gave him
A support for his practice.

"He prostrated to them in parting
And left for Tibet.
Because he had accomplished fleetness of foot,
He traveled as fast as a bird in flight.
Because he had accomplished invisibility,
No one saw him.

When he reached the barrier at the border,
Vairochana entered the samadhi
Of overpowering the experience of others.
He paid the border tax in gold powder
And was let through the barrier.

In one month he reached Tibet.
He met with the dharma king Trisong Detsen,
And the omniscient abbot and master.[32]
A great feast was held with all gathered there.

Then the king invited Vairochana
To the upper story of the central temple
And asked him to teach dharma.
At first Vairochana taught
The *Sutra on the Deeds of Awakening.*
Then he taught The *Vinayagama a*nd so on.

He stayed there, turning various dharmachakras.
The Indians were displeased

And discussed him.
They decided to send three runners
To Tibet to spread slander.

Three atsaras were sent and reached Tibet.
They went into the crowd at a market
And said, "The king of Tibet is a fool!
He has been deceived!

"The man who calls himself Vairochana
Is a demonic evil magician!
He didn't bring back the authentic dharma for
    which he was sent!
He has brought to Tibet
A lot of ruinous, evil spells.

"If he is permitted to teach,
All Tibet will fall to ruin!
If he is prevented and killed,
Your land will be saved!
The dharmaraja of India is benevolent.
For Tibet's sake we three were sent."

The queen met with all the Bönpo ministers.
They said, "It is true!"
And rewarded the three atsaras.

They discussed the situation
And assembled before the king, saying,
"This Vairochana is a deceiver, a liar.
He did not get the holy dharma for which he was sent!

"He has returned with all sorts
Of ruinous, evil spells!
The king of India, in his supreme benevolence,
Knowing that Tibet would be ruined,
Sent messengers fleet of foot.

"They told us, 'This Tibetan boy didn't get dharma!
He learned evil spells!
Don't let this bringer of disaster live!
Kill him!'
As he will harm Your Majesty,
Pass sentence on him now!"

The king replied,
"None of this is true!
It is slander born of jealousy.
Arrest those three messengers!
Throw them into a dungeon!
Vairochana is my guru.
Whose law is it to punish the innocent?"

Furious, the king attacked his ministers with
    a cudgel.
They were shocked and, having no choice,
    they fled.
The Buddhist minister Dorje Trelchung gathered
    his men
And arrested the three atsaras.

They were cast into a dungeon
With fetters binding their limbs.

Under the king's authority,
They were left alone to suffer for seven days.

Then they were released,
Their mouths stuffed with ashes.
The queen and the Bönpo ministers were displeased.

They said to Dorje Trelchung, the minister from Tsang,
"You have concealed these demonic spells
And tormented those with good intentions!
If evil befalls all Tibet and our king,
You will be to blame!"

The minister replied,
"I have done what the king commanded.
I did nothing out of personal dislike.
If there is something wrong with obeying our king,
You must all be His Majesty's superiors!
I am not afraid of you, even if you kill me!
I am going to tell the king of all this."

The queen and all the Bönpo ministers conferred
And decided, "We will burn Vairochana alive.
If the king protects him, we will restrain him
And take our vengeance!"

The queen said,
"We must kill Dorje Trelchung!"
The other ministers said,
"It would be wrong to kill him.
He was telling the truth when he said

That he had just obeyed the king's command."

After coming to an agreement
They went into the king's presence and said,
"This Vairochana is a bringer of disaster.
There is no point in letting him live.
Kill him now!
Your Majesty, listen to us.
If you don't, great evil will ensue!
King, think about it!"

Trisong Detsen thought,
"There is no other way left to me.
I must lie to them, and say yes!"

He said, "If it is certain that he is a master of demons,
Place him in a sealed copper vessel
And cast it into the water!"

The queen and ministers were delighted.
They brought two large copper pots to the king
And said, "He must be cast into the water
At this very instant!"

The king replied, "Given that he is a caster of evil spells
That bring disaster, it would be more auspicious
To cast him into the water after sunset."

They all said, "It is so!"
They discussed it further among themselves.
When they had come to unanimous agreement,

The Lotus Garden

The king consulted the Buddhist ministers
Takna Dongzik and Dorje Trelchung.

They captured through deceit a foreign beggar,
Gave him many precious things,
And made sure he would not die.
Vairochana taught him how to escape from the water.

They prayed for his well-being
And placed him in the copper vessel.
It was sealed with the royal seal
And made water-fast.
A great drum was beaten.
The queen and ministers gathered.

The king proclaimed, "We send off this bringer of disaster
With one-sided drums and thighbone trumpets,
With a ransom offering, ashes, and various grains!
Let him not remain!
Cast him into the water!"

Terrified, the beggar began to cry.
The queen, who knew the sound of Vairochana's voice,
Became suspicious and said,
"Before casting this copper vessel into the water,
We should open it and look within!"

But Takna Dongzik had great influence. He said,
"Vairochana was sealed in there this morning
Out of the fear that he might escape.
It is now evening!

If you wanted to look inside,
You should have come this morning.
But you didn't!
Fool, don't you recognize the magician's voice?
If we open it now,
He might cast all kinds of spells and escape!
It would be better to leave it sealed."

The king said to the queen, "You liar!
Your real purpose is to help this bringer of disaster,
This magician, to escape!
I am not going to bring disaster on myself,
So why do you doubt where there is no cause for doubt?
I swear to you, with Draktsen as my witness,[33]
That this is Vairochana!"

Saying that, the king slapped the queen's face.
At that, everyone was sure it was Vairochana.
They dispatched the ransom offering,
Threw ashes, and gave a great cry.

The copper vessel, with the beggar inside it,
Was cast into the water.
Through the prayers of Vairochana and the king,
The copper vessel was carried by the current to Oka,
Where it came to rest on the riverbank.

Everyone from the area gathered.
They opened it and found within it the beggar,
Alive and very healthy.
He was taken out of the water,

Built his home there, and came to be known as
The Merchant Brought by Copper in the River.
The dharma king was clever.

From *The Lotus Garden, A Biography of Vairochana,* the ninth chapter: "Slander of His Dharma Teaching, and the Averting of Obstacles."

Chapter Ten

Slander by the Bönpo Ministers and Exile to Gyalmo Tsawarong

Then Vairochana thought,
"If I remain in Tibet,
There will be no benefit to beings.
My Indian masters said to me,
'If you possess instruction,
Wherever you go is the realm of disciples.
Don't teach profound dharma.
Be prepared to run.'
This is the time of which they spoke.
Having spoken to the king,
I should go."

He packed the *Sutra on the Deeds of Awakening,*
The *Sutra on the Purification of Lower States,*
And the *Sutra on the All-Encompassing View.*

He said to the king,

"Great dharma king, listen to me.
You have cared for me since my childhood.
Maintain your faith, interest, and respect
For this holy dharma.

"The queen and ministers, blessed by maras,
Hate and are jealous of authentic dharma.
This precious, profound dharma that I have translated
Will not disappear. My gurus have predicted this!

"But it is not the right time.
I am going elsewhere.
Your Majesty, be well!
We will meet again someday.
Then we will be able to teach and hear holy dharma."

Displeased, the king said,
"Don't say such things!
You don't have to teach dharma to the unreceptive,
But I have faith and enthusiasm.
Please teach me profound dharma!"

Vairochana was touched by this,
And said to the king, "Very well."
Out of the fear that others would see,
A cavity was carved into the side of a column.

Vairochana hid inside it.
He did not teach the king dharma during the day,
But practiced rasayana.
In the evening, when the king came to receive dharma,

He would bring Vairochana a meal.

Eventually the queen came to wonder,
"Each night the king disappears.
He must have taken another woman!"
Anxious, she followed the king,
And saw him serving Vairochana,
Who was teaching dharma.

Queen Margyenma beat a great drum,
Causing all the ministers
To be assembled at one time.

The queen said to them,
"All of you assembled here, listen!
The person cast into the water was another!
The magician was concealed!
I have seen him!

"He is teaching the king
All sorts of ruinous things!
Capture him now!
We must slit his throat with a sharp razor
Where we can all see it done!"

They were all in agreement with this,
And went to see the king.
Enraged, Tara Lugong said,
"King of Tibet, you deceive yourself!

"This man, who claims to be translating dharma,

Is teaching you a lot of evil spells!
Your sworn word is meaningless!
You cast a beggar into the water!

"You have concealed this monk,
This bringer of national disaster!
You have suppressed the Bön protectors
Relied upon by all your ancestors!

"Kill this caster of spells right now!
Look at what he has wrought
In the name of dharma!
Decorate your palace with his head and limbs!"

The king couldn't tolerate this,
And was inflamed into a rage, and said,
"The king's authority should be accepted by all!
'Minister' means someone who obeys the king.
If the tail rises higher than the head,
We are no more than bugs or ants.
Vairochana is a guru who teaches authentic dharma!
If you want killing, I will kill you!"

The king took up his sword
Called Slices the Shoulders of Wild Men.
He turned as red as lungs dripping blood.
The queen and ministers were intimidated
And unable to say a word.
They stood there as if paralyzed.
Tara Lugong prostrated himself in fear.

The king arose from his throne
And picked up earth and stones to throw.
Margyenma and the ministers fled in fear.
King Trisong went into Vairochana's presence.

Crying, he said to him,
"My only beloved son!
My wretched queen and ministers
Know of your presence here!
What shall we do?"

Vairochana said to the king,
"My honored father, Your Majesty!
In order to satisfy them,
Do whatever they ask.

"When there is no karmic cause,
There is no way to get what you want.
If there is powerful karma at work here,
And the residue of habit,
I am not afraid of being killed.

"I will have no regret even if I die!
Although the dharma I have practiced
Is no use to them now,
I pray that it may help beings in future lives."

The king would not allow Vairochana
To submit to execution, and said,
"My only karmic son, Vairochana!

How could I leave you
In the hands of those butchers?
Yet there is a great obstacle to dharma.
Go to a place not too distant from here.
There will be a way for us to meet later."

They discussed this a great deal.
Then the king had the great drum of law beaten,
Summoning the queen and ministers.
He said, "Since you bringers of ruin
Hate from the depths of your hearts
Vairochana, who is an authentic guru,
I will banish him. He will not remain here.

"You, Tara Lugong!
Since you have opposed me
To the point of treason,
You are demoted from the status of a minister!
You will henceforward be a commoner,
A herdsman of horses!"

Then the king offered Vairochana, without anyone seeing,
Ten measures of gold dust and a golden bowl,
    and said to him,
"My only son, where do you wish to go?
I will exile you to wherever you choose, so tell me!"

Vairochana answered,
"I have karma in Gyalmo Tsawarong in the east.
I will go there."
Carrying his dharma texts,

He began his journey.

The king had Tara Lugong brought before him.
He subjected him to various punishments
And forced him to work as a herdsman of horses.
After that no one dared speak to the king
Without thinking very carefully first.
Those who counseled him with care
Remained happy.

From *The Lotus Garden, A Biography of Vairochana,* the tenth chapter: "Slander by the Bönpo Ministers and Exile to Gyalmo Tsawarong."

Chapter Eleven

Turning the Dharmachakra in Gyalmo Tsawarong

Then the great translator Vairochana
Went to Gyalmo Tsawarong
Through his accomplishment of fleetness of foot.
In a valley filled with trees and flowers
A band of monkeys were gathered to play.
He came to that uplifting and delightful place.

For seven days he accomplished the goddess Kurukulle.[34]
Birds and monkeys brought fruit,
Which they offered to the great master Vairochana.
He stayed there, teaching the monkeys
The *Precious Ushnisha Tantra on Purifying Lower States.*

The king of that region liked to capture wild animals alive.
Seven hunters appeared one day, chasing a deer.
They saw the monkeys listening to dharma
And offering fruit to Vairochana.

They tried to catch some of the monkeys
And present them to the king,
But Vairochana paralyzed the seven hunters.
Unable to move, they remained there.
That place came to be known as Paralysis.

At dawn, the seven hunters
Were able to return home.
They told the king what had happened.

He said, "He doesn't sound like a human being.
He might be our local deity, Yutse.
Go look for him and, if he's still there, bring him."

The ministers sent a hundred soldiers
Ordered to fulfill the king's command.
When they went to look,
They saw what had been reported.
They proclaimed the king's command
And told Vairochana that he must accompany them.

Vairochana said, "You are all
Deserving of compassion!
You cover your bodies with armor!
You hold stones and weapons in your hands!

"You take me to be your enemy,
Yet I am not afraid of you!
However, because there is a residue
Of karma from the past,
You may serve as my escort, not my enemies!

I will go to see King Doksher Nakpo."
He went with the soldiers.

That king's palace was called Blazing Agate.
It was vast and beautiful.
In it lived the ruler, Doksher Nakpo.
He had seven wives but no sons,
And was attended by a hundred junior ministers
And ten senior ministers.
He was very wealthy and powerful and had many servants.

They left Vairochana outside one of the palace gates,
And told the king what had happened.
He consulted his ministers.
He decided, "Whatever he is,
He is unlike others!
It is difficult to know whether he is good or bad.
First we must test him to find out what he is."

They cast him into a pit of lice
And left him there for three weeks.
Then they looked at him and found
That he had come to no harm.
He was radiant, healthy, and impressive.

They told the king of this. He said,
"He is amazing, superior to others.
I have no heir; perhaps he is my destined son.
Ask him his story and try to find out what he is."
The minister Ngawang Palden went to Vairochana
And asked him, "What is your name?

What is your family? From where have you come?
Where were you going? What do you want?"

Vairochana answered,
"My name is Vairochana. My family is Vairochana's,
The family of body. My clan is the Apo Dong.[35]
I come from Tibet. I have nowhere else to go,
And there is nothing I want other than this:
This place is the realm of my disciples,
Because of previous karma.
I have come here to teach authentic holy dharma."
The minister told the king
What Vairochana had said.

The king said, "This man is greater than all others.
He is either a god or a magician.
Cast him into a pit of vicious frogs for seven days.
If he survives, he is my destined son,
And I will obey his every command
And carry him on my head!"

They cast Vairochana into the frog pit.
After seven days the king, queens,
And ministers went to look.
Vairochana's body was utterly unharmed.

The Buddha Vairochana decorated his head.
All the turtles faced away from him.[36]
Amazed, they brought him out of the pit.
The king was remorseful and frightened.

He cried a great deal, saying,
"To have done such awful things
To an actual buddha, an emanation of Vairochana!
I have bad karma!"

He bowed his head to Vairochana's lotus feet,
And venerated him as his guru.
The king offered his crown, robes, and boots
    to Vairochana.
He invited him to the upper story of his palace
And served him all sorts of food.

On the eighth day of the month Saga,
The king, queens, ministers, and subjects assembled.
They offered a mandala of gold,
Silver, and various jewels.
They made this request for the teaching of dharma:

"Oh Vairochana! Oh supreme vidyadhara!
Had we tried to find you, we would have failed!
Yet through previous karma we have met you,
The greatest of men! We pray that you teach
Authentic, profound holy dharma;
That you ripen and free us all,
King, queens, ministers, and subjects;
And that for the rest of our lives you stay here
And never leave!"

The master answered, "King, ministers, and subjects, listen!
In my eighth year I went to Tibet.

In my fifteenth year I traveled to India.
I translated a lot of authentic, profound dharma into
    Tibetan.

"I thought that land would be steered by dharma,
But because the impure queen and ministers decided
That they liked Bön and disliked dharma,
They slandered me. I was banished.
If you will all not act like them,
I will ripen and free you with dharma.

"In the past, in this place,
I was born as an ascetic,
A pratyekabuddha called Purnajnana.
I placed my saffron robes in sunlight,
And allowed birds to eat the lice that emerged.

"As a result, I was cast into the louse pit.
When I was born as a foolish sheep,
I ate many of the frogs here alive.
As a result, I was cast into the frog pit.

"Karma, causation, doesn't just disappear!
Therefore, all of you, be very careful
In your actions, because of their results!"
Saying that and other things,
He taught a great deal about causation.

Then he recruited translators of dharma:
Yudra Nyingpo, whom he had predicted;[37]
Yudra Paldrön, the king's daughter;

And other intelligent persons of good family.
Seven of the many assembled became translators:
Daö Zang, Tsewang Chögyal,
Mani Dönyö, Punapala,
Kunga Dvaja, Prajnavajra,
And Suryamanga, the son of a minister.

They trained as translators and became skilled.
At first they translated the *Vinayagama,*
The *Vinayottara,* the *Purification of Lower States,*
Emptying Hell to Its Depths, the *Amoghapashatantra,*
The *Stainless Lotus Sutra,* and innumerable other sutras.

They also translated secret mantra,
Including the *Hundred Thousand Tantras,*
Prana, chandali, and the Great Perfection
Of the mind class, the mother and son expanse class,
And much of the instruction class.

They translated seven types of rasayana,
A hundred types of instruction,
Forceful mantra, and magic.
All the men and women of Tsawarong assembled.
They praised and venerated Vairochana.

From *The Lotus Garden, A Biography of Vairochana,* the eleventh chapter: "Turning the Dharmachakra in Gyalmo Tsawarong."

Chapter Twelve

The Building of Temples by the Dharma King Doksher Nakpo

All the people of that land were delighted
And took Vairochana as their guru.
They all listened to holy dharma.
They were all filled with dharma
Of sutra and mantra, of ripening and liberation.[38]

Eventually the king was struck by illness.
His ministers conferred and went to see
    the master.
They addressed him,
"Great vidyadhara, honored Vairochana!
Our dharma king, Doksher Nakpo,
Is unwell, struck by illness.
What are the causes and conditions of his illness?
Does he or does he not face an obstacle?
Please perform whatever service
Is needed to cure his illness."

Vairochana answered,
"The results of actions are powerful.
Because he initially punished me,
The king has been struck by illness.
If I perform the ritual of *Emptying Hell to Its Depths,*
It will help."

The ministers, pleased, returned to their homes.
Vairochana performed the ritual of
Emptying Hell to Its Depths.
The king prostrated himself
And recited the hundred syllables.

He offered a hundred thousand incenses,
Butter lamps, and feast cakes,
As well as an immeasurable variety
Of other offerings.

He dispensed food to all the poor in his realm
And gave them half the wealth in his treasury.
He built one hundred and eight stupas
Surrounding his palace,
Employing many builders in their making.

Vairochana bestowed the empowerment
And instructions of *Single Ornament Vajrasattva.*
Three days later the king was freed from illness.
His queens, ministers, and subjects were relieved.

Then the king said,
"Great master, honored Vairochana!

Through your compassion,
Tsawarong has been placed in dharma.
You have saved my life by averting this obstacle."

The king praised Vairochana's kindness at length,
And then offered him an excellent and complete
Set of monastic appurtenances,
Including the upper and lower robes
And a begging bowl, saying,
"It would be wonderful if this land
Could hold both a monastic community
And a tantric community.
I will create these two communities
From a few of the many who will apply.
I pray that you give them vows and samaya."

Vairochana replied, "Good. I will."
Three hundred monastics,
Led by Yudra Nyingpo;
And seven hundred and twenty-five mantrins,
Led by Düdül Dorje, received respectively
The vows and samaya of sutra and mantra.

The king had them live in the right
And left wings of his palace.
Then the dharma king Doksher Nakpo
Summoned his senior and junior ministers.

He said to them, "Now, through the kindness
Of the master Vairochana,
Two dharma communities, one of sutra

And one of mantra, exist here.
We should next build a temple."

He discussed this with his ministers,
Who said, "That would be wonderful!
Ask Vairochana to design it.
We will build whatever he tells us to,
And employ all the court."

So the king asked Vairochana,
Who tamed and blessed the site through ritual.
On Saturday, the day of the Snake,
The eighth day of the third summer month
In the Male Earth Dragon Year,[39]
The construction of the foundation began.

A temple was built for each of the two
Communities of sutra and tantra.
The work was finished without obstacle
In the Male Metal Horse Year.[40]

The monastic residence was called Jewel Garden.
The accomplishment hall of the mantrins was called
Garden of Great Bliss Where Maras Are Conquered
Through the Accomplishment of Yamantaka.

From *The Lotus Garden, A Biography of Vairochana,* the
twelfth chapter: "The Building of Temples by the Dharma King
Doksher Nakpo."

Chapter Thirteen

The Creation of Meditation Supports by the Dharma King Doksher Nakpo, and the Flourishing of Beings' Benefit

The monastic temple called Jewel Garden
Had five stories and was constructed
According to the custom of India.
The tantric temple called Garden of Great Bliss
Where Maras Are Conquered had three stories
And was built according to Chinese custom.

After they were built, Doksher Nakpo thought,
"Although the temples and the dharma
That is the support of speech have been created,
Supports of body and mind have not.
I must ask Vairochana and create images!"

He enlisted smiths of gold and silver
And molders of images from copper and iron.
Vairochana created the designs
And the king had the images made.

The principal image in the lower hall
Of the monastic residence was a statue
Of Shakyamuni made of gold, one story tall.
Surrounding it were life-size statues
Of the eight close sons, made of silver.

There were also statues of the sixteen elders
And of the twelve pratyekabuddhas;[41]
One depicting Vairochana;
And images of the four great kings.

Above that, in the central temple called Unmoving
Was an image of the buddha Vairochana
Made of gold and copper, along with
The other four victors and the sixteen bodhisattvas.[42]

Above that, in the hall of Unchanging Immortality,
The principal image was of the protector Amitayus.
With it were the life deities of the five families
And the twenty-one Taras.

Above that, in the hall of Great Compassion,
The principal support was an image of him
With a thousand arms and eyes and eleven faces.
With it were images of Great Power
And Dispels All Obscurations,[43]
Eight stupas, and relics of the Buddha.

Above that, in the hall of meditation,
Was an image of Amitabha one story high,
With Avalokita and Vajrapani on his right and left,

Along with the protector Maitreya, Vajrasattva,
And the victors of the five families.

The murals in the monastic residence depicted
The thousand buddhas of this fortunate kalpa,
The previous lives of Shakyamuni,
The eight sugatas of medicine,[44]
Each of the life deities a thousand times,
The scholars of India, and Vairochana's life.

The principal support in the lower hall
Of the tantric temple was of Guru Rinpoche,
Made of copper, one story in height.
On his right and left were Shantarakshita
And Vimalamitra, along with life-size
Statues of the eight noble vidyadharas.

There were images of the eight names of Guru Rinpoche;
Of the teachers of the two doctrines; of the three bodies;
And of his forceful form, Blazing Wisdom.[45]
The murals there depicted Guru Rinpoche's life
In detail and the record of the king Doksher Nakpo.

In the middle hall the principal statue
Was of the victor Yamantaka, surrounded by
His retinue of one hundred twenty-five deities.[46]
Written on the walls were tantras of Manjushri.

In the upper hall the principal statue
Was of Vajrapani, surrounded by his retinue:
The fierce ones of the four families,

The ten wrathful ones, and the five garudas.
Written on the walls were tantras of Vajrapani,
And one hundred and eight dharmakaya stupas.

Vairochana was pleased, his wishes fulfilled.
The teachings of both sutra and mantra
Had spread and flourished there.

From *The Lotus Garden, A Biography of Vairochana*, the thirteenth chapter: "The Creation of Meditation Supports by the Dharma King Doksher Nakpo, and the Flourishing of Beings' Benefit."

Chapter Fourteen

The Fulfillment of His Wishes and the Consecration of the Temples

Then colleges of teaching, accomplishment, and meditation
Were founded in the temples of sutra and mantra.
Vairochana sang this song
About the achievement of beings' benefit:

"Such happiness! Such joy!
When I die, I will have no regrets.
I went to India and studied
With many scholars and siddhas.

"I retrieved authentic dharma.
I returned to Tibet.
They banished me, but I am unharmed.
Beings' benefit has increased.
I am happy!

"In Gyalmo Tsawarong in the east

I met a king emanated by Vajrapani
And lit the beacon of authentic,
Profound dharma.
My learning has not been wasted.
I am happy!

"Here in Tsawarong,
The realm of my karmic disciples,
The sunrise has dispelled
The darkness before dawn.
This land has become virtuous.
Everyone has been ripened and freed.
When I die, I will have no regrets.
I am so happy!

"In a land without virtue
Profound dharma has been translated.
Supports of the body, speech, and mind
Of the victors have been made.
Colleges for the teaching and accomplishment
Of sutra and mantra have been founded.
I have served the teachings.
I am so happy!"

The dharma king Doksher Nakpo thought,
"It would be good if the temples
And supports of body, speech, and mind
Were consecrated, and if a dharma protector
For each one was appointed."
He requested this, and Vairochana replied,
"Consecration is easy.

To establish supports for dharma protectors,
Protectors' halls need to be built."
So it was done.

In the monastic temple images of
Shri Mahakala, Shri Devi, and Tseringma
With her four sisters were made.
The supports were placed.
The deities were acclaimed.
Accomplishers were appointed.[47]

In the mantrins' temple, images of
Ekajati, Rahula, Vajrasadhu,
And Yama of Activity were made.
Their supports were placed.
They were acclaimed.
Accomplishment groups were formed.

On a Sunday in the third autumn month
Of the Male Iron Horse Year,[48]
Under the constellation Victory,
The ritual of consecration began.

The king, queens, and all the ministers were there.
People of all statuses throughout the land,
Hearing of a great celebration,
Put on their jewelry, got on their horses,
Washed with cool water,
And came there with smiling faces.

The king decorated an elephant

The Lotus Garden

With six articles of jewelry and rode it,
Singing all kinds of songs of joy.
The queens and ministers rode horses,
Attended by three hundred and six
Armored soldiers on horseback.

They circumambulated and gazed at the temples.
When Vairochana cast the flowers of consecration,
A rainbow appeared in the sky, thunder resounded,
And flowers fell like rain.

There were many such good signs.
Especially, the temples were filled with light.
Everyone saw the deities actually dissolve
Into their supports. Everyone was amazed.

They all began to play in their delight.
The king emptied one of his treasuries,
Using it all for outer, inner, and secret offerings
To the two great temples of sutra and mantra.

There was a tremendous feast and celebration.
So much was given to everyone there
That none remained poor afterward.
For seven days they all stayed there,
Singing and dancing out of joy,
Racing their horses, and competing in archery.

From *The Lotus Garden, A Biography of Vairochana*, the four-
teenth chapter: "The Fulfillment of His Wishes and the Consecration of the Temples."

134

Chapter Fifteen

The Concealment of Treasure in Gyalmo Tsawarong and the Dharma King Doksher Nakpo's Acceptance by Guru Rinpoche's Wisdom Body

Then Vairochana thought,
"Beings' benefit is increasing.
I must now accomplish
The state of a supreme vidyadhara."

He went to a place in Tsawarong
Called Conch Mountain.
Remaining there for three months,
He achieved siddhi.
Then an invitation came from the king,
And Vairochana went to the palace.

Doksher Nakpo prostrated himself
And offered a mandala, saying,
"Honored Vairochana, knower of
All that transpires in the three times!

The Lotus Garden

"You have planted the doctrine here
And built temples and colleges
Of teaching and meditation.
You have created supports
Of body, speech, and mind.

"I am wealthy and my court prospers.
But I have no sons, and I worry
What will happen in the end.
Vairochana, you possess many means.
I pray that you, in your compassion and kindness,
Bestow means to ensure that my dynasty
Will not end with me and that the tradition
Of dharma will not be lost."

Vairochana replied with true words:
"Dharma king Doksher Nakpo!
Mundane things never end in permanence.
There is no way to make your dynasty last.
You will not be here forever.

"Your dynasty will survive
For three generations after your death.
Then a king named Youth will appear.
His seven sons will scatter the kingdom
Through dispute over the succession.

"This land will be split into many fiefs
Ruled by many lords.
They will even fight over the possession
Of the two great temples of sutra and mantra.

"They will divide among themselves
  The supports of body, speech, and mind.
  There is no way to prevent this;
  It is due to past karma."
The king became miserable, and said,
"Is there truly no way to stop this?
  Will everything I've done go to waste?"
He wept and covered his head.

Vairochana said to him,
"Listen, great dharma king!
  No dynasty or kingdom lasts forever.
  If you wish dharma to last and spread,
  Conceal extremely profound treasures in the earth."

The king replied,
"Excellent, excellent, intelligent Vairochana!
  So that dharma may last for a long time,
  Conceal it as treasure.
  I will provide all that is needed.
  Think kindly of future beings' benefit.
  Please prevent the disappearance of holy dharma.
  Preserve it as treasure."

Vairochana said, "This is excellent!"
They prepared all the materials
For the writing of treasure scrolls:
Paper and inks of gold, silver, copper, and vermilion;
Treasure containers of the same metals;
Charcoal made from horns and corpses
And various things that burn;

Lead solder, birch bark, and medicinal powders;
Powdered gold, silver, copper, and iron;
And various clays for the outer vessels.

Vairochana, Doksher Nakpo,
And Yudra Nyingpo wrote them.
Some were written in Tibetan script;
Some in symbol script;
Some in Indian scripts;
And some in Kashmiri script.

Anointed with the scents of the six excellent medicines
And other herbs, they were placed in their containers.
Treasures of wealth were concealed as well.
Various jewels, various silks,
And all varieties of things that are precious
Were taken from all parts of the royal treasury
And placed in containers made of precious materials.

Statues and stupas made by Vairochana's hands;
Statues of protectors and supports of their minds,
Qualities, and activity, all made magically
By the emanated king of smiths, Drupay Lodrö,
And blessed by the protectors themselves,
Placed in containers and sealed indestructibly;
The king's most precious jewel;
The queens' most precious jewelry;
Vairochana's cloak, hair, robes, cup, and begging bowl:
These and other things were set aside
As treasure for future benefit.

Then Vairochana, the king, the queens, and
  the ministers
Traveled throughout the kingdom of Tsawarong,
Looking for thirty-eight particular significant places.
They caused blessings to descend on those places
And they blessed the ground.

They concealed the profound treasures
And entrusted them to their protectors.
They invited the sugatas, who actually dissolved into
And remained within the treasures.

While the king and ministers were at ease,
A ray of light emerged from Vairochana's heart,
Pointing to the west.
The vidyadhara Guru Rinpoche, Padmasambhava,
Appeared in the company of dakinis of the
  four classes.

Vairochana said,
"King and ministers, prostrate yourselves!
This is my guru, Guru Rinpoche.
All who see or hear him are ripened, freed,
And placed on the path."

Delighted, the king and ministers bowed
And received empowerment.
Guru Rinpoche said, "King Doksher Nakpo!
Throughout your previous lives
I have blessed you!"

Guru Rinpoche then taught them many instructions
On outer, inner, and secret liberation.
The king and his ministers were liberated
By hearing them.

From *The Lotus Garden, A Biography of Vairochana*, the fifteenth chapter: "The Concealment of Treasure in Gyalmo Tsawarong and the Dharma King Doksher Nakpo's Acceptance by Guru Rinpoche's Wisdom Body."

Chapter Sixteen

His Preparation for Returning to Tibet After Establishing Gyalmo Tsawarong in Dharma

Then the master Vairochana, the king,
And the ministers returned to the palace.
The queen Aryakumala felt unwell;
It was evident that she was pregnant.

Many rituals were done for her benefit,
And she eventually gave birth to a prince.
The king and ministers were delighted
And held a great celebration.

Vairochana bestowed a life empowerment
On the prince and named him
Chögyal Sönam Deutsen.
Then a merchant in the king's service named Gyurti
Returned to the palace from Tibet.

Vairochana asked him,

"Are there still Indian scholars and siddhas in Tibet?
Is authentic, profound dharma still taught there?
Are the great abbot Shantarakshita
And Guru Rinpoche still in Tibet?
What are they teaching?"

The merchant answered,
"Guru Vairochana, all of Tibet is happy.
The Indian mahapandit Vimalamitra is there.
Many are being trained as translators.
The bodhisattva and Padmasambhava
Are at Samye, but I have not heard
What they are teaching."

He told Vairochana these and other things.
Vairochana, pleased, said to Yudra Nyingpo,
"Don't stay here. Go to Tibet.
Find out what pandits and translators are there
And what dharma they are teaching.
Wear ordinary clothing; be a hidden yogin.
Don't tell anyone anything.
Go without anyone knowing where."

Yudra Nyingpo went to Tibet.
He went to the upper hall
In the central temple at Samye
And wandered through the crowd.
He talked to everyone and heard
That Vimalamitra was there.
He went to Vimalamitra's dharma class
And stood up in the midst of the assembly.

He shouted, "KAKAPARI!" and stood there.
Vimalamitra answered, "Sangha sign dissolved."
Delighted, he laughed and gazed at Yudra Nyingpo.
The king and the other disciples were worried.
Yudra Nyingpo vanished into the crowd.

The king asked the master Vimalamitra,
"What is the meaning of KAKAPARI,
Which that foreign monk shouted at you?"

Vimalamitra answered,
"He was speaking to all of us.
To me he was saying, 'Why are you teaching
Dharma for the lowest capacity
And not dharma of the mahayana?'

"To you disciples he was saying,
'You with bad karma and incorrect views
Who mistake virtues for flaws
Are unworthy of the mahayana.
How sad to see the infantile
Listening to dharma!'
That is what he meant, king and disciples."

The king commanded,
"He must be learned. Find out where he went,
And bring him here."
The Tibetan ministers invited Yudra Nyingpo
To the upper hall of Samye.
Vimalamitra, pleased, asked about Vairochana.

Yudra Nyingpo answered,
"He has placed all of Gyalmo Tsawarong in dharma.
His activity and benefit of beings flourishes."
The abbot, the master, Vimalamitra, and the king
Were all pleased to hear this.

Then Yudra Nyingpo translated dharma.
He knew everything that Vairochana knew.
He translated the eighteen mother and son tantras
Of the mind class of the Great Perfection.

Then he returned to his own land from Tibet.
He entered the palace called Blazing Agate.
He went into Vairochana's presence
And told him all that had happened.

Vairochana was pleased and said,
"Yudra Nyingpo, son of my heart,
I am delighted by your journey to Tibet,
And by your confirmation of what we had heard.

"Among the many scholars and siddhas of India,
Vimalamitra is the best.
As he is my guru,
I am pleased that he has gone to Tibet.

"Padmasambhava of Uddiyana
And the bodhisattva Shantarakshita
Are peerless, so I am pleased that
They have not left Tibet.

"King Trisong Detsen loves dharma.
I am pleased that his wishes are being fulfilled.
I have now placed this land in dharma.
Beings' benefit is accomplished.
I shall soon go to Tibet."

King Doksher Nakpo was displeased by this and said,
"Vairochana, my guru,
Your kindness in benefiting beings is beyond
    measure.
I pray that you not leave, but stay here.
There is no difference between the three lands
Of Tibet, Gyalmo Tsawarong, and China
In the benevolence of their rulers
Or the size of their courts.

"There are still wild places at our borders.
Please, Vairochana, go to them
And establish China in dharma.
There is no guru here other than you.
In Tibet there are many pandits and siddhas.
If there is the sun, one can do without the moon."

No matter what the king said,
Vairochana did not consent. He said,
"If there is no one who can be tamed,
There is no one who can tame them.
Eventually I will have to go to China,
But now is not the time. I'm going to Tibet.
I won't be there long; we'll meet again."

He taught the king how to rely on a guru.
The first way to rely on a guru is externally.
Receive dharma that ripens and frees,
And engage in pleasing service.

The second way to rely on a guru is internally.
Accomplish whatever is commanded,
Offer your body and possessions,
And carefully protect recollection and alertness
As you protect your eyes.

The third way to rely on a guru is secretly.
Meditate on the guru above your head.
Pray and receive the four empowerments.
At the end, he melts into light
And is indivisibly mixed with your mind,
Like two things with one flavor,
Like water poured into water.
Nurture the point of suchness,
Liberation upon arising.

The fourth way is to mix the clear lights at
    the time of death.
The self-arisen nature, absolute truth, the
    primordial expanse,
Is the unity of the guru and your mind.
In their inseparability, transfer your consciousness
To the expanse of dharmakaya,
Without concept and free of elaboration.

Vairochana gave many other instructions,

And prepared to go to Tibet.
The king beat the drum of council,
Summoning his ministers.

He said, "The master is not staying here!
He must go to Tibet."
No matter how hard they tried to convince him to stay,
They were unable to stop him from leaving.

The king commanded,
"We will escort him to Tibet
And make offerings in gratitude.
I and all my ministers and court
Will escort him all the way to
Yarmotang in eastern Tibet.
Yudra, I will send you and whoever else
In the dharma communities of sutra and mantra
Is dear to Vairochana to Tibet with him."

The ministers were in agreement on this
And sent fast runners throughout the kingdom
To summon all the people.
They proclaimed,
"It is certain that the master is not staying here,
And that he is going to Tibet.
Offer whatever you can and escort him."

Everyone gathered like clouds.
Vairochana performed an empowerment of
The *Peaceful and Wrathful Ones*
Who Empty Samsara to Its Depths.

A golden throne piled with nine brocade cushions
Was set up in Blazing Agate, the royal palace.
Vairochana sat on this.
To his right sat Yudra Nyingpo on three cushions.
The other translators sat on a single cushion each.
To Vairochana's left sat the king on a silver throne.
His chief minister, Kongrong Litsa Trobar,
Sat on three cushions, the other ministers on one.
The rest were seated according to rank.
Behind, on the left, were all the mantrins.

The king said, "Most kind Vairochana,
You lit the beacon of dharma in this dark land.
You have enabled me to gather the accumulations
And to encounter profound dharma.
You have placed my queens, ministers, and court
   in dharma."

Having spoken at length of Vairochana's excellent
   kindness,
The king offered him five hundred and one measures
   of gold dust,
Seven thousand silver ingots, a hundred horses, a
   hundred mules,
And a full load of tea to be carried by each of them.

The queens offered all their precious jewelry.
The ministers and common subjects offered
   whatever they could,
And prepared to accompany Vairochana as an escort.

Vairochana said to them, "King, ministers, and
    subjects, listen!
I am not a guru who desires material wealth.
I will conceal as treasure for future benefit
This gold, this silver, and the queens' jewelry.
The rest I don't need; please take it back."

No matter how much they tried to convince him
To accept it, he would not.
The king offered his spirit-turquoise and all his jewelry,
Vowing, "If you don't take this,
It will be the same as killing me!"

Vairochana accepted it and concealed it
At Good Helmet Red Rock.
He divided the rest of the gold and silver
And concealed it in the thirty-eight great places.

From *The Lotus Garden, A Biography of Vairochana,* the six-
teenth chapter: "His Preparation for Returning to Tibet After
Establishing Gyalmo Tsawarong in Dharma."

Chapter Seventeen

His Journey from Tsawarong to Tibet

Then the dharma king Doksher Nakpo,
The queens, ministers, five hundred attendants,
And all the people of Tsawarong assembled.
Vairochana, wearing the saffron robes of a vinayadharin,
Mounted the steed called Rekpa Dongnak.
All the male and female members
Of the dharma communities of sutra and mantra
Wore their respective robes and carried aloft
Banners, parasols, and cymbals.
They all escorted Vairochana as far as Palyul Kongyaktang,
Where he miraculously erected a hundred and
     eight stupas.
He also concealed many fine treasures.

Vairochana said, "King, ministers, subjects, all of you!
In the future I will return this way, but for now I
And my best disciple, Yudra Nyingpo,

Must continue our journey together."

They asked his permission to accompany him
All the way to Yarmotang in eastern Tibet,
But he would not consent.
The king, the ministers, and the others,
Filled with regret and weeping,
Returned to their land.

Vairochana and Yudra went to Tibet.
On the way they concealed a hundred and eight treasures.
They reached Samye while the great celebration
Of the tenth day was in progress,
And walked into the assembly
Of all the translators and pandits.

The great abbot, Guru Rinpoche,
Vimalamitra, the dharma king,
And all the translators and pandits
Were delighted.

From *The Lotus Garden, A Biography of Vairochana,* the seventeenth chapter: "His Journey from Tsawarong to Tibet."

Chapter Eighteen

His Achievement of Beings' Benefit in the Land of Li

Then Vimalamitra and Vairochana
Translated many tantras of outer,
Inner, and secret mantra.

The bodhisattva and Yudra Nyingpo
Translated shastras on vinaya and sutra.
Padmasambhava and Namkai Nyingpo
Translated the profound path of means:
Channels, winds, and chandali.

Each of the other pandits and siddhas
Worked with one of the other translators.
They translated all the sutra and mantra
That existed in India.
They preserved the authentic Bön tradition,
And suppressed its perversion.

At that time the queen and all the Bönpo ministers,
Seeing Vairochana, felt guilty, ashamed, and nervous.
The Buddhist ministers and subjects were all delighted.
Whenever they saw Vairochana's face,
They placed his feet on their heads.

The combined teachings of sutra and mantra
    flourished.
The dharma king Trisong Detsen's hopes were
    fulfilled.
The abbot and the master remained in Tibet.
The king offered a great mandala in gratitude.

Vimalamitra went to China.
The other pandits returned to their own parts of India.
They were escorted to the border of Tibet and Nepal.
Vairochana settled in Yamalung.

He did whatever the king wanted.
Eventually the time came for the New Year celebration.
During it the king was killed in a horse race.
The abbot, the master, and all the translators
    assembled.
They performed the ritual for the dead from
The *Peaceful and Wrathful Ones*
Who Empty Samsara to Its Depths.

The throne was presented to Mutik Tsenpo,
Who, like his father, Trisong Detsen,
Governed the kingdom according to dharma,
Establishing it in happiness.

The great master went to Chimpu near Samye.
The bodhisattva remained in the upper story
    of Samye.
The great, learned translator Vairochana
Went to the forest called Tsukrum Barwa in Yerpa.
He remained in the samadhi of the Great Perfection.

Eventually, in the land of Li, its king, Chandrajnana, died.
He left no sons but one daughter,
The princess Jangchub Drönma.
She had faith in dharma and respect for gurus,
And was an emanation of White Tara.

She sent three messengers to Vairochana,
Who said, "We were sent to invite you."
They presented him with the letter of invitation
And an accompanying offering.

Vairochana went to see both the abbot and the master,
Told each of them of this, and asked them what to do.
Guru Rinpoche told him, "The time has come.
If you go immediately, beings' benefit will flourish."

Vairochana obediently went to Li.
The royal palace was called Ratnamani.
It was magnificently appointed
And immeasurably vast.

Vairochana was brought to its upper story,
Served various delicious beverages,
And offered a precious mandala.

The princess Jangchup Drönma,
Along with a gathering of her ministers and subjects,
Prostrated themselves in joy and devotion.
They placed Vairochana's feet on their heads.

The princess said,
"Supreme vidyadhara, master Vairochana!
Although holy dharma has spread to this land of Li,
Gurus who have achieved authentic liberation
    are rare.

"My father, the late king, is gone.
Since he had no sons, I now rule.
Because my body is female
I am considered inferior
And should not have to rule,
But because I have not gathered the accumulations,
I have fallen into the samsara of being a ruler.

"Vairochana, teacher of the definitive meaning,
In your compassion accept me!
Introduce me to the self-arisen!"
She begged him in that way repeatedly.

Vairochana replied, "Worthy Jangchup Drönma,
    listen to me!
Your body in this life is female,
But you are of good family.
You possess karma and are interested in authentic
    dharma.
The path to awakening exists for women too.

Princess, I will ripen and free you!"
He taught her all the tantras and agamas of the
    mind class.
She asked, "Are mind and awareness the same
    or different?
Are wisdom and consciousness the same thing?"

Vairochana answered, "Jangchub Drönma, listen!
What moves is mind.
Its nature is awareness.
If primordial purity is realized,
They are said to be one.
Wisdom is the primordial purity of consciousness.

"When resting evenly,
That abiding in emptiness
Is the recognition of dharmakaya.
The lucidity is said to be sambhogakaya,
The movement nirmanakaya.

"Those three are one in the expanse.
If you remain in equality without ever straying,
That exhaustion of dharmas,
That transcendence of the intellect,
Is svabhavikakaya."

He taught her a great deal of liberating dharma
    like that.
Jangchup Drönma experienced the point.
She recognized self-arisen wisdom and was liberated.
Thirty-seven others with karma were liberated as well.

Vairochana taught the very profound dharma of the
    Great Perfection.
Sixty people attained the rainbow body in that land.
The land of Li became a field of disciples.

From *The Lotus Garden, A Biography of Vairochana*, the eighteenth chapter: "His Achievement of Beings' Benefit in the Land of Li."

Chapter Nineteen

His Manifest Buddhahood, the Conclusion

Then the translator Vairochana thought,
"My benefit for beings in this land is complete.
I will return to Tibet and Gyalmo Tsawarong."

To the princess and all her ministers and subjects
He said, "Your wishes are now accomplished.
There are still disciples of mine in Tibet.
So I am going there."

No matter how earnestly the princess tried to
    convince him,
He would not consent to remain.
They then offered him much gold and silver, and
    many jewels.
He returned to Tibet and met the abbot and the master.

He received the messenger sent by Doksher Nakpo,

Who requested him to go to China and Gyalmo
    Tsawarong
In order to care for beings destined to be his disciples.
A letter to this effect and an accompanying offering
Were placed in his hands.

He asked the master and showed him the letter.
Guru Rinpoche told him,
"It is now time for you to tame beings in China.
If you go there, I will accompany you inseparably."

So seven went to Gyalmo Tsawarong:
Vairochana, Namkai Nyingpo, Yeshe Tsogyal,
Langchen Palseng, Gyalwai Lodrö,
Palgyi Wangchuk, and Yudra Nyingpo.

They cared for those who remained there
To be accepted as disciples.
Then they went to China,
Where they concealed many profound treasures
And established that land in dharma.

Guru Rinpoche's wisdom body was always with them,
And was seen by a few of the fortunate.
They stayed in Tsarong and China for five years.
This biography was written during that time.

When Doksher Nakpo died,
They performed his funeral service
And placed him on the path to liberation.
They enthroned his son and entrusted the kingdom to him.

Vairochana taught dharma that ripens and frees, and
    made aspirations.
Although the son asked him to remain, he refused.
The people of Tsawarong presented many offerings
And escorted him all the way to Yarmotang.

Vairochana and his companions went to the upper
    hall of Samye.
They met with the abbot and the master
And conversed with them.
Then Vairochana went to Yamalung Red Rock.

He completed the practice of the Great Perfection
And achieved buddhahood
With no aggregates remaining.[49]

From *The Lotus Garden, A Biography of Vairochana*, the
nineteenth chapter: "His Manifest Buddhahood, the
Conclusion."

SAMAYA! Sealed! Sealed! Sealed!

I, Yeshe Tsogyal, completed this biography for the future benefit of beings. I wrote it in magic script and concealed it as treasure. May it be found by a worthy person with karma!

GUHYA! KHATHAM!

This was received as siddhi by Chime Tennyi Yungdrung Lingpa.

Notes

1. The "fivefold excellence" mentioned here is the nirmanakaya equivalent of the five certainties of the samboghakaya. In the samboghakaya context, they are the certain teacher, the principal samboghakaya buddha Vairochana; the certain place, the realm of Akanishtha; the certain retinue, bodhisattvas of the tenth level; the certain dharma, the Mahayana; and the certain duration, until samsara is emptied of beings.

2. The tenth day of the waxing phase of each lunar month is associated with male deities and, in particular, Guru Rinpoche. The tenth day of the waning phase is associated with female deities. On both days, tantric practitioners gather to perform an offering ceremony called a ganachakra, or "gathering circle."

3. Either 863 C.E. or 923 C.E.

4. "Khampas" are inhabitants of Kham, eastern Tibet.

5. Vairochana, which means "All-Illuminating," is the name of the victor of the buddha family, the principal samboghakaya buddha. Since Vairochana the translator was an emanation of this

buddha, he was given the name Vairochana.

6. "The eight freedoms and ten resources" are the principal characteristics of a human birth with access to dharma. They are presented in Gampopa's *Jewel Ornament of Liberation* and other sources.

7. Because we are told neither how old Vairochana is at the time of telling his story nor the year's element, we don't know which Ox Year is intended. The possibilities include 813, 835, 857, and 879 C.E.

8. A "rishi" is a person so upright that he or she always speaks the truth. A "siddha" is someone who has achieved either a degree of awakening or magical power.

9. A LA LA HO is an expression of joy and wonder. SIDDHI PHALA means "attainment result," and can in this context be understood to mean "attainment will result." SIDDHI JNANA means "attainment wisdom," and can in this context be read as "the attainment of wisdom."

10. Although the description of Vairochana's birth in this chapter is sometimes written in the first person and sometimes in the third, the chapter's setting makes it clear that Vairochana is telling the story to his gathered disciples. Because it is stated at the biography's end that it was written by Yeshe Tsogyal in consultation with Vairochana, and because it is mostly written in the third person from the second chapter onward, it has been translated in the third person from here onward, and quotation marks are therefore omitted in the remaining chapters except where the story includes dialogue.

11. See note 7.

12. About five miles.

13. TRI RAM HUM appears to be the number three, the syllable of

fire, and the syllable of mind. AVARANA means "obscurations."
PRAVESHAYA can mean "to spread out, to diffuse," or, as in this
case, "to dispel." PHAT has the connotations of splitting, sepa-
rating, and interrupting. JNANA means "wisdom." PRAJNA
means "discernment." AVESHAYA is used to mean "to gather, to
dissolve into, or to enter." HO represents joy. Collectively, these
mantras indicate that Manjushri is burning away or removing
Genjak's obscurations and causing wisdom to enter into him or
arise within him.

14. *Lhasang,* "cleansing of the gods," is a ceremony in which fra-
grant juniper and consecrated substances are burned producing smoke that is believed to purify the environment and its
inhabitants of the pollution caused by immorality and other
forms of contamination. This helps the performer purify his or
her obscurations and also benefits all who are touched by the
smoke.

15. At different places in the biography, Vairochana's mother is
called Drenka Zadrön, Drenkaza, and other variations of her
name. These all refer to the same person.

16. See note above. Affixing the suffix *kyi,* "happy," to someone's
name is one of several ways of turning the name into a term of
affection in Tibetan. The word *ga,* "joy"; the word *ya,* "good";
and the syllable *lu* are also used in this way. It appears that *kyi*
is usually used with women's names. There also appear to be
regional differences in the use of these nicknames.

17. According to Jamgön Lodrö Taye's short biography of
Vairochana in his book *Lives of the Hundred Treasure-Revealers,*
Vairochana was given the name when he received monastic
vows from the abbot Shantarakshita. His name in full was
Vairochanarakshita, which literally means "Vairochana
Protector." According to the same source, he was one of the "sev-
en tested men," who were the seven young men carefully
selected to be the first recipients of monastic vows in Tibet.
Their ability to keep their vows was taken by Shantarakshita

as an indication that Tibet was a fit land for the vinaya.

18. A meditation belt is used to help maintain proper posture during meditation practice, especially during meditation on the channels and winds and during the practice of the expanse class of the Great Perfection, with which Vairochana is particularly associated.

19. "The view of permanence" is the belief in the continuous existence of an independent, indivisible, and unchanging self. In a wider sense, it can refer to the belief in absolute existence. "The view of termination" is the belief that experience ceases at death. In a wider sense, it can refer to the belief in absolute nonexistence.

20. A "water-moon" is the reflection of the moon in water.

21. "The threefold world" can refer to either the three levels of existence (celestial, terrestrial, and subterranean) or the three realms (the desire realm, the form realm, and the formless realm).

22. The word *samaya* refers to the vows of tantric practice, which include obedience. Here Vairochana is commanding the obedience of the lake goddesses by proclaiming that they are bound by samaya to obey him. This either means that they have previously received samaya vows or that they are about to. The text implies the second meaning.

23. This appears to be the point at which they receive samaya.

24. The word *atsara* is believed to be a corruption of the Sanskrit word *acharya*, which can mean "a master teacher," and is nowadays used to refer to the academic degree of "Master." In Tibetan writings, *atsara* is used to refer to itinerant Indian yogins, much the way the word *sadhu* is used nowadays.

25. The meaning of this is uncertain.

26. Ekajati, the principal protector of the Great Perfection teachings.

27. The nine vehicles of Buddhism are the shravakayana, the pratyekabuddhayana, the bodhisattvayana, the kriyayogayana, the upayogayana, the yogayana, the mahayogayana, the anuyogayana, and the atiyogayana. There is nowadays a great deal of information available about them in English in the published teachings of various eminent teachers of the Tibetan traditions.

28. "Chiti, yangti, and the complete great end" are three further divisions of atiyoga, the Great Perfection.

29. Translated in the style of our text, this could mean, "Most precious guru, please give me the wondrous, resultant attainment, the wisdom of dharma!"

30. "Rasayana" is the practice of sustaining oneself through the consumption of progressively more and more refined and subtle means of nutrition, culminating with the sustenance of awareness itself. "Chandali" is one of the main aspects of the path of means.

31. The teachings of the Great Perfection are divided into three classes: mind, expanse, and instruction.

32. The abbot is Shantarakshita. The master is Padmasambhava. Often they are listed, along with Trisong Detsen, as "the abbot, the master, and the dharma king."

33. Draktsen is a protective deity of Tibet.

34. A deity associated with the power of attraction.

35. Vairochana uses the word *family* here to mean "buddha family," and *clan* to mean "human clan."

36. The mention of both frogs and turtles implies that the pit contained a variety of reptiles and amphibians, many of them

presumably poisonous.

37. According to *Lives of the Hundred Treasure-Revealers,* Yudra Nyingpo was the rebirth of Vairochana's former traveling companion, Tsangngon Lekdrup.

38. "Ripening" refers to empowerment, which ripens one's being. "Liberation" refers here to the instructions through which one achieves liberation.

39. Either 848 or 908 C.E. is intended.

40. Either 850 or 910 C.E.

41. "The eight close sons" are the eight bodhisattvas: Manjushri, Avalokiteshvara, Vajrapani, Maitreya, Akashagarbha, Kshitigarbha, Samantabhadra, and Sarvanivaranavishkhambin. "The sixteen elders" are the sixteen disciples of the Buddha appointed by him to protect his teachings. "The twelve pratyekabuddhas" are twelve sages who achieved the state of an arhat without, in their final lives, relying on the teaching of others.

42. The sixteen bodhisattvas are the eight male and the eight female bodhisattvas of the Vajradhatu mandala.

43. Vajrapani and Sarvanivaranavishkhambin.

44. The eight Baishajyagurus, or "teachers of medicine."

45. "The teachers of the two doctrines" are Shakyamuni and Padmasambhava. "The three bodies" are Amitabha, Avalokiteshvara, and Padmasambhava. "The eight names" and Blazing Wisdom are all forms of Padmasambhava.

46. Yamantaka is the wrathful form of Manjushri.

47. It is traditional that consecrated images of protectors are used as supports for the daily accomplishment of those protectors.

48. See note 40.

49. This means that he achieved the rainbow body.

Acknowledgments

We wish to gratefully acknowledge the inspiration of Jamgön Kongtrul Rinpoche and his gracious contribution of the foreword to this book, and to express our gratitude to the Jamgön Kongtrul Labrang for providing the photograph of Rinpoche.

We also express our appreciation to Daia Gerson for her professional assistance as copyeditor; to Mary Young for her expert final proofing of the text, typography, and design; to Naomi Schmidt for her technical assistance, and to all who offered assistance and support.

Yeshe Gyamtso, Peter van Deurzen, and
Maureen McNicholas—KTD Publications

His Eminence, the Fourth Jamgön
Kongtrul Rinpoche, Lodrö Chökyi Nyima

Jamgön Kongtrul Labrang

Pullahari is the main seat of His Eminence, the Fourth Jamgön Kongtrul Rinpoche, Lodrö Chökyi Nyima. The age-old tradition of prayers, rituals, training, and education of monks continues in the monastery as does the three-year Mahamudra retreat. Facilities for study and retreat by lay Buddhist practitioners are available throughout the year at the Rigpe Dorje Study Center.

Pullahari Monastery & Retreat Centre
PO Box 11015, Kathmandu, Nepal
Tel.: +977 (1) 4 498196
Email: pullahari@jamgonkongtrul.org

Tsandra Rinchen Drak
Palpung, Derge, East Tibet
The Main Seat of the Jamgön Kongtruls since Jamgön Kongtrul Lodrö Thaye; it is one of the twenty-five sacred sites in Eastern Tibet

Kagyu Tekchen Ling Monastery & Retreat Centre
PO Lava Bazaar, Kalimpong
Distt. Darjeeling, West Bengal, India

Karma Triyana Dharmachakra

Karma Triyana Dharmachakra (KTD) is the North America seat of His Holiness the Gyalwa Karmapa, and under the spiritual guidance and protection of His Holiness Ogyen Trinley Dorje, the Seventeenth Gyalwa Karmapa, is devoted to the authentic representation of the Kagyu lineage of Tibetan Buddhism.

For information regarding KTD, including our current schedule, or for information regarding our affiliate centers, Karma Thegsum Choling (KTC), located both in the United States and internationally, contact us using the information below.

Karma Triyana Dharmachakra
335 Meads Mountain Road
Woodstock, NY, 12498 USA
845 679 5906 ext. 10
www.kagyu.org
KTC Coordinator: 845 679 5701
ktc@kagyu.org

KTD Publications

GATHERING THE GARLANDS OF THE GURUS' PRECIOUS TEACHINGS

KTD Publications, a part of Karma Triyana Dharmachakra, is a not-for-profit publisher established with the purpose of facilitating the projects and activities manifesting from His Holiness's inspiration and blessings. We are dedicated to gathering the garlands of precious teachings and producing fine-quality books.

We invite you to join KTD Publications in facilitating the activities of His Holiness Karmapa and fulfilling the wishes of Khenpo Karthar Rinpoche and Bardor Tulku Rinpoche. If you would like to sponsor a book or make a donation to KTD Publications, please contact us using the information below. All contributions are tax-deductible.

KTD Publications
335 Meads Mountain Road
Woodstock, NY, 12498 USA
Telephone: 845 679 5906 ext. 37
www.KTDPublications.org